THOMSON

COURSE TECHNOLOGY

Professional ■ Technical ■ Reference

Digital Painting Fundamentals with

Corel®

painter™ X

ISBN-10: 1-59863-404-6
ISBN-13: 978-1-59863-404-4
Library of Congress Catalog Card Number: 2007923310
Printed in the United States of America
08 09 10 11 12 BU 10 9 8 7 6 5 4 3 2 1

Publisher and General Manager, Thomson Course Technology PTR:
Stacy L. Hiquet

Associate Director of Marketing:
Sarah O'Donnell

Manager of Editorial Services:
Heather Talbot

Marketing Manager:
Heather Hurley

Acquisitions Editor:
Megan Belanger

Marketing Assistant:
Adena Flitt

Project and Copy Editor:
Kim V. Benbow

Technical Reviewer:
D. A. Winder

PTR Editorial Services Coordinator:
Erin Johnson

Interior Layout:
Shawn Morningstar

Cover Designer:
Mike Tanamachi

CD-ROM Producer:
Brandon Penticuff

Indexer:
Sharon Shock

Proofreader:
Gene Redding

THOMSON
★
COURSE TECHNOLOGY ™
Professional ■ Technical ■ Reference

Thomson Course Technology PTR, a division of Thomson Course Technology
25 Thomson Place ■ Boston, MA 02210 ■ http://www.courseptr.com

For "Gypsy Roz"—artist, dancer, model, and friend.

Acknowledgments

This is the book I've been wanting to write for many years, and I'm grateful to Stacy Hiquet and the entire staff at Thomson Course Technology for helping to make it happen—especially Megan Belanger who got me off to such a good start and Kim Benbow who steered me to the finish line, holding my hand and wiping my brow when necessary. Thanks to Heather Hurley in marketing, as well as the team for graphic design and layout. For technical editing, I have Darren "Daz" Winder to thank, and I'm also grateful to Brandon Penticuff for designing the CD interface.

Thanks to the friends and family members who allowed me to use their likenesses for educational purposes. A big thank you goes to Joseph Schaller for the terrific photos of Gypsy Roz in her belly dancing outfit, and for helping me celebrate completion of the book by taking me to see *Spider-Man 3* at an IMAX theatre.

I want to thank the folks at Corel Corporation for continuing to develop and improve Painter, the Natural Media software of choice for digital artists. A very special thank you goes to Wacom Company for setting the bar so high with regard to pressure-sensitive graphics tablets and for giving me so many freebies over the years.

Finally, I'm deeply grateful to Carole McClendon, my agent at Waterside Productions. Thanks for believing in me and for all your work behind the scenes.

About the Author

Rhoda Grossman is the author of numerous books and tutorials on the creative uses of Painter and Photoshop, most recently *Fun with Photoshop Elements*. She has taught basic drawing as well as computer graphics techniques at several schools in the San Francisco Bay area and has earned a reputation for lively and humorous presentations. Rhoda became a "pixel-packin' mama" in 1990 and uses pixel-based software for commercial illustration and cartooning, as well as fine art projects. She has successfully transferred traditional figure drawing skills to the computer, and brings her Mac PowerBook and Wacom tablet along to life drawing workshops where she specializes in quick gesture drawings. As "Rhoda Draws a Crowd," she creates digital caricature entertainment for trade shows and conventions. A member of the National Caricaturist Network (NCN), Rhoda is a pioneer in using digital media for live caricature at events, and she has won several awards from her professional colleagues. Visit her Web site at www.digitalpainting.com.

Contents

Part II Beyond the Basics

6 Graphic Techniques............................103

7 Mixed-Up Media.............................123

Introduction

Welcome to Digital Drawing and Painting

Digital Painting Fundamentals with Corel Painter X will get you started with Painter X or the two previous versions. It provides step-by-step instruction for using the basic software and hardware that are the industry standard for pixel-based drawing and painting: Corel Painter and a Wacom graphics tablet. (If you're not sure what a tablet is or what pixels are, see the Appendix in the back of this book.) Exercises and projects will give you increasing control of tools and techniques. You will acquire and sharpen the skills needed for working in any medium, such as eye-hand coordination and drawing what you see. But there's more to digital art than just knowing how to make a series of marks on an electronic canvas: you will also be introduced to traditional art concepts such as composition, line quality, contrast, and focal point.

With digital art, there's no need for the labor of stretching canvas and preparing a surface to accept pigment. You won't need to replenish dried-up tubes of paint or replace broken chalk and worn-out brushes. Your clothes won't get spattered with ink, you will never inhale toxic fumes, and your hands will stay clean. (For artists who would actually miss the messiness of a traditional studio, Wacom might be working on making a pressure-sensitive leaky pen that smells like turpentine!) You can save every version of a painting as it develops. Your digital paper won't wrinkle, your colors won't fade, and with 32 levels of Undo, there's no such thing as a mistake. As for storage space, hundreds of drawings and paintings can fit into a few cubic inches of CDs or your hard drive.

A Little History

Unleashed in the early 1990s, Painter brought forth a new era for pixel-based digital graphics. Painter was the first "Natural Media emulation" program, created for artists by artists! With this software, along with the newly developed pressure-sensitive graphics tablets to replace the mouse, artists could now begin to work comfortably at the computer. Painter has matured over the years, surviving the transfer from its parent company, Fractal Design, to Corel Corporation, and remains unrivalled for its capacity to imitate virtually any natural medium. (It also has a consider-able number of bells and whistles for creating effects that go way beyond what can be produced "naturally.")

When Painter was released, I was in the right place at the right time (for a change), creating digital caricatures as a booth attraction for computer graphics trade shows. I painted with Photoshop then, but when I saw what Painter could do, I knew what my future looked like (for a change). I still rely on Photoshop for image manipulation, but Photoshop's Brush tool is anemic compared to Painter's robust array of brush styles and controls. Incidentally, these two applications have become more and more compatible with each other over the years. You can create an image in either program, then open it in the other for additional work, using the best features of each. Taken together, Photoshop and Painter are the Dream Team for pixel-pushers.

I've written books and tutorials on both Photoshop and Painter for about a decade, and I've taught both digital and traditional art skills in the classroom during most of that time. I began developing a curriculum for teaching traditional art fundamentals in a digital environment about five years ago. This book represents the culmination of that effort so far.

Who Needs This Book?

If you are in one or more of the following groups, this book is for you.

- Traditional fine artists and illustrators getting ready to "go digital," or at least willing to give it a try.

- Novice or intermediate users of Corel Painter and Wacom tablets, with little or no art background.

- Photoshop users who want to enhance their creativity with the "other" pixel-based program.

- Hobbyists and digital Sunday painters of all ages who might need a bit of hand-holding to get started or go to the next level in their enjoyment of this medium.

Others who would be well advised to choose this book as their introduction to Corel Painter are impatient users who don't want to sit through an interminable explanation of every nook and cranny of the program before they're allowed to get their feet wet. In this book, you're invited to jump in and splash around almost immediately. If you enjoy the instant gratification of your creative impulses, Painter is just the ticket! Using a Wacom tablet with Painter is so intuitive, young children can get the hang of it in a few minutes. I gave a hands-on workshop at ZEUM, the Art and Technology Center for Children in San Francisco, and these kids could create awesome stuff—if their parents got out of the way.

When traditional artists get a glimpse of the enormous capabilities of Corel Painter, they can usually overcome any fear of technology that might stand in their way—it happened to me 16 years ago. I was a technophobic artist/illustrator who became suddenly intrigued with digital art in middle-age and managed to create a new career path with my "beginner's mind" and the courage to explore unknown territory. I am now an official tour guide into that territory. I'm still not really a "techie," and that makes me an ideal trainer for people who need a little hand-holding to break into digital art. This book will help traditional artists transfer their skills to the computer. It will also show folks who think they have no "talent" that they can learn the basics…then it's just practice, practice, practice. I am convinced that if you are computer literate, you can learn to draw and paint digitally—if you can set aside fears, insecurities, and negative judgments about your readiness and self-worth. (Oops, is my background in psychology showing?)

No prior experience with Painter or other graphics applications is required. Oh, yes—you'll need a Wacom tablet, unless you really prefer drawing with a bar of soap or a hockey puck.

What You Will Learn

Although the word "drawing" doesn't appear in the title of this book, drawing is an essential foundation for painting. Drawing ability, like many skills, is a combination of natural aptitude and training. We don't expect a pianist to simply sit down and play a concerto without years of study and practice, including scales and fingering exercises. Lesson 1 provides exercises and the graphic equivalent of musical scales to prac-tice eye-hand coordination, control, and technique. Use these exercises for a few minutes before each session to warm up and loosen up before you begin to work. You might never play the piano, but you'll be able to draw one.

Personal fulfillment and More

Sadly, public schools don't offer much to nurture creativity. Art (and, to a lesser extent, music) is neglected and discounted as an esoteric pursuit reserved for the rare person who is "talented" from birth. Most people go through life thinking they have no such talent, while the truth is, they simply haven't learned some basic skills and concepts that can be mastered with practice. Creative expression is not only important for personal fulfillment, but also a valuable element in a healthy society.

Lesson 2 introduces basic drawing techniques that you will continue to use throughout the book. If you already have skill using traditional art materials, you'll find it easier to master digital media. If you don't have traditional drawing or painting expertise, you can begin to develop it here. Drawing and painting techniques can be learned and improved by anyone at any age.

Famous drawing teachers like Betty Edwards (*Drawing on the Right Side of the Brain*, Tarcher, 1999) agree that the ability to draw is based in large part on the ability to see accurately. In these lessons, you will be encouraged to develop your ability to look critically at your subject, whether it's a still life or a nude model, and observe the shapes, lines, textures, tones, and proportions that are essential to making a successful drawing. With practice, you will be able to improve your ability to see your subject and interpret what you see.

The projects presented in these lessons begin with simple assignments and gradually become more challenging. They cover a wide range of subjects and techniques, including

- Tracing a photo
- Sketching a still life
- Painting a landscape
- Portraits and self-portraits
- Figure drawing
- Cloning a photo in different styles
- Abstract painting
- Illustration and graphics techniques
- Experimental animation
- Mixed media caricature

I'll also give you the opportunity to peek under the hood at Painter's brush engine occasionally, showing you how the controls work so you can customize your brushes.

This book is not an exhaustive encyclopedia of Painter, so keep your user guide handy. I didn't even try to present every aspect of the program, in order to keep the focus on drawing and painting. Our main course is exploring the Natural Media brushes, with special effects and image manipulation as side dishes. By the time you finish all the projects in all the lessons, from soup to nuts, you will have digested most Painter techniques and had a nibble of many others. You'll probably find some brushes and tools more to your taste than others. And if you're still hungry for more instruction, there are resources in the Appendix.

How to Use This Book

Lessons 1, 2, and 3 (in that order) will give you enough of the fundamentals to get you off and running. After that, you can feel free to jump around and do what looks interesting at the moment. Within a lesson, it's a good idea to start with the first project and work down, but even that isn't absolutely required.

Each project is liberally illustrated with images at various stages to keep you on track. Screen captures of dialog boxes, menus, and palettes will help you navigate the program and choose options. These screenshots were all made on a Mac, but the difference between them and the Windows version is merely cosmetic. In any case, I'll give keyboard commands for both Mac and PC. For example, Command/Ctrl means use the Command key if you're on a Mac, the Ctrl key if you use Windows. Including the keystroke equivalent every time I mention a command will be awkward, so I added a list of the most popular keyboard shortcuts in the Appendix.

This book focuses on Corel Painter X, but users of versions 8 and IX have not been ignored. With very few exceptions, these versions are practically identical. You'll be given tips along the way, pointing out any significant differences, such as new features or options available only in Painter X. Photoshop users will find that a great many Painter tools, palettes, and commands are the same or similar to what they are accustomed to. In a few special cases, I couldn't help mentioning how each program handles a task differently, but you won't find extensive comparisons between Painter and Photoshop here. That's beyond the scope of this book.

The Appendix at the back of the book has some suggestions for customizing Painter preferences to suit the way you like to work. Use the default settings for a while, if you're not sure about these choices. Some basic terms and definitions can be found there, along with other handy bits of information. There are resources for images, fonts, and printing, and even a little free legal advice. I also list other books and publications to help you develop as a digital artist, so take a look back there once in a while.

What's on the CD-ROM?

Here's where you'll find the source images needed for all projects, organized by lesson number or by subject categories. There are photos of people, places, and things mostly shot by me (so I could deduct my camera as a business expense). Some of the images were donated by family and friends. In addition to the specific images I use in each lesson, many more photos are provided for you to choose from or to use in your own projects. You are encouraged to use your own source images for some projects, especially for the self-portrait.

Corel Painter provides ways to organize your favorite tools and art materials. The Palettes and Libs folder on the CD contains custom palettes and libraries to accompany specific projects, making it easier for you to jump right into a lesson without having to rummage around searching for the recommended brushes, colors, and other items. You'll learn how easy it is to create your own custom palettes and libraries, too.

The Rhoda Portfolio folder has samples of my digital art created in successive versions of Painter, spanning about 15 years. These show my use of several styles, showcasing the range and versatility of Painter. You'll see some illustration assignments, as well as personal projects, portraits, abstract painting, cartooning, and experimental caricatures created live at trade shows and other events. (All files on the CD-ROM can also be downloaded from the Course Technology Web site at www.courseptr.com.)

But enough about me. I'll see you in Lesson 1.

PART

I

The Basics

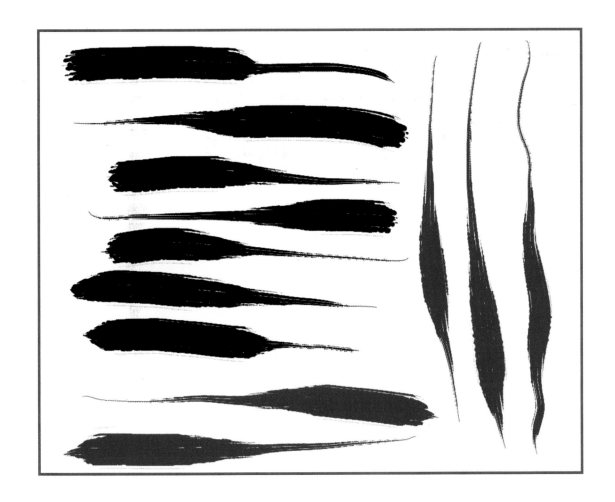

1 Welcome to Painter

If you read the Introduction, then you know this book addresses versions 8, IX, and X of Painter, Corel's powerful software for Natural Media sketching and painting. You are also aware that a pressure-sensitive tablet is necessary for working effectively with Painter—any Wacom tablet will be fine. If you didn't read the introduction, I admire your eagerness to get right to the main course. But, trust me, there are some tasty appetizers in those opening remarks. Lesson 1 will still be nice and warm when you get back.

I made these chapter opener scribbles with just a few of the brush variants available in most versions of Painter. In just a few minutes, you'll be able to create digital scribbles as good as this! So launch your Painter program, and let's get started.

You'll need a blank canvas to work on. When the Welcome screen comes up (version IX or X), choose Create New Document. If you don't get a Welcome screen, just choose File > New (Cmd/Ctrl+N). The New dialog box, shown in Figure 1.1, lets you enter height, width, and resolution for the image. We'll use 72 dpi most of the time, so you'll be able to see the whole image on screen without scrolling, and you can work faster. (Pixels and resolution are explained in the Appendix.)

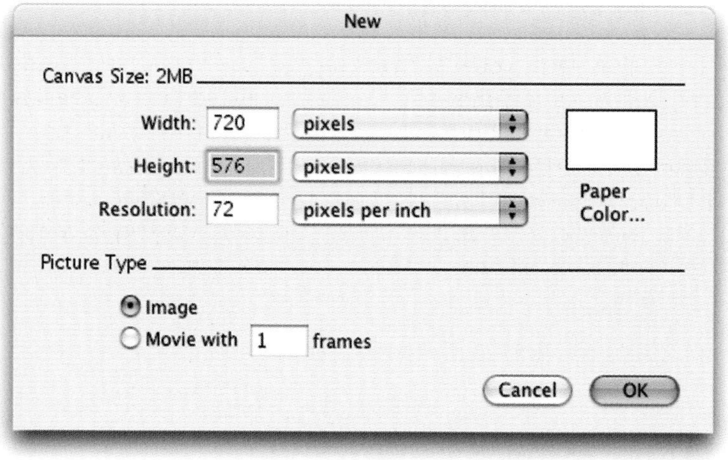

Figure 1.1

Choose size and resolution for your new canvas.

Getting Acquainted

In addition to your canvas, the Painter workspace consists of several palettes offering brushes and other art supplies, as well as special features and commands. All palettes are listed in the Window menu and can be organized any way you like. (We'll talk about customizing palettes later.) You'll see the vertical Toolbox on the left side of your screen. Make sure the Brush tool is selected, as in Figure 1.2. If all you want to do is draw and paint, you can ignore all the other choices in the Toolbox for quite a while.

Working with Painter, you will have only one tool in your hand—the Wacom pen. Hold it as shown in Figure 1.3. Avoid touching the lever on the side of the pen's barrel (it has click functions that won't be useful while you're drawing). This model is the Intuos 3 with a 6" x 8" active area, my preferred size. Pressure sensitivity enables you to control the width and/or opacity of your stroke by varying how hard you press the tip of the pen to the tablet as you work.

Figure 1.2

The Brush tool lets you make your mark.

Figure 1.3

Wacom tablet and pen.

The marks you make with your Wacom pen can imitate virtually any traditional art material. Traditional (analog) tools for drawing and painting include a wide variety of pencils, pens, brushes, and sticks. They differ greatly in the kinds of marks they can make and the type of material they can mark: paper, canvas, or boards, with various kinds of surface texture. You'll choose your digital "brush" with the Brush Selector Bar in the upper-right corner of the Painter workspace. It has two sections: one for the category and the other for the specific variant within that category. Figure 1.4 shows the Design Marker (20 pixels size) in the Felt Pens category as the current "brush." Each category has a distinctive icon, and the shape of the variant's tip is also shown. That black rectangle means the Design Marker has a chisel shape.

When Is a Brush Not a Brush?

When it's a pencil, or a pen, or a piece of chalk! Painter uses the term "brush" in a generic way to refer to everything used for drawing and painting on your digital canvas.

Figure 1.4

The Brush Selector Bar shows the current category and variant.

Let's Scribble

Click on the Brush Category section to see the long list of options. Figure 1.5 shows most of them. Look over the list to get a feel for how many choices you have, but don't let that scare you! Move your cursor to Pens and click to choose that group. Now click on the Brush Variant section and choose Scratchboard Tool, as in Figure 1.6. This is my favorite pen variant for line drawing and cartooning. Make some strokes and squiggles on your canvas, changing the pressure and speed of your stroke.

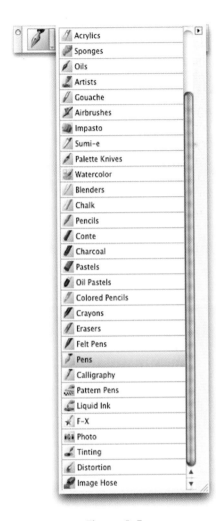

Figure 1.5

There are 36 brush categories in Painter X.

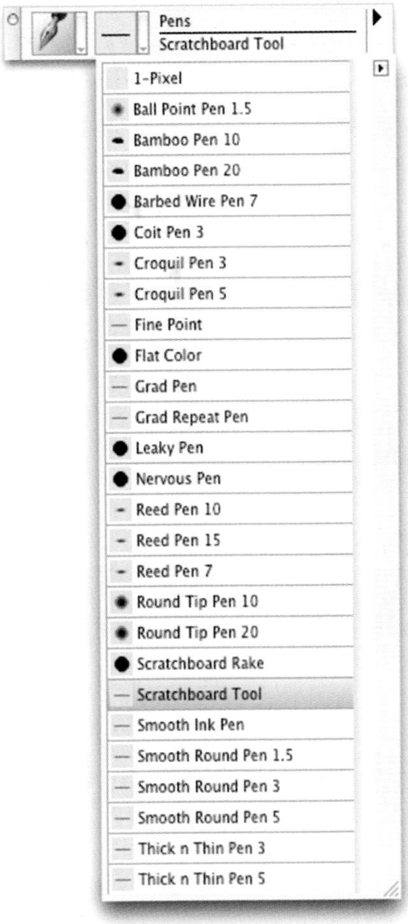

Figure 1.6

Choose the Scratchboard Tool from the Pens group.

Figure 1.7 includes some Scratchboard Pen lines I made in the scribble sampler at the beginning of the lesson. We expect pens to make smooth lines that might have thick and thin variations based on the tip shape or pressure applied.

Figure 1.7

Scratchboard Tool practice.

I Love the Pressure!

Did your pen strokes respond to pressure variations? Even more important, did the lines appear where you wanted them? Use the following tip to confirm that your Wacom tablet is functioning properly.

If the pen strokes required more pressure than you're comfortable with, or (on the other hand) if the pen seems too sensitive to pressure changes, you can customize the tablet's sensitivity within Painter. Click on Corel Painter in the menu strip and find Preferences > Brush Tracking. Make a stroke in the rectangle shown in Figure 1.8. Painter will automatically adjust to your touch! It's a good idea to do this every time you launch Painter and whenever you change the way you work. Now try some more pen strokes on the canvas, and see if that helped.

Test Your Tablet

Make sure the tablet is mapped to your computer screen by doing the "two-point test." Touch the point of your pen to any corner of the active area of the tablet and notice that your cursor shows up at the corresponding corner of your screen. That was one point. (If that didn't work, you're in trouble—see the Wacom tablet section in the Appendix.) Now lift the pen away from the tablet (don't drag it!) and touch it to the opposite/diagonal corner. If the cursor shows up in the new position, you're good to go. If not, see the Appendix.

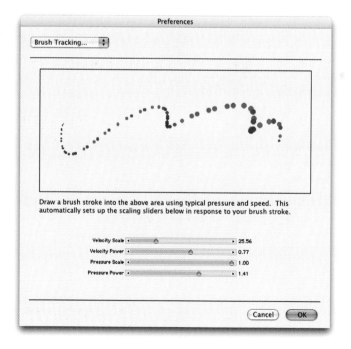

Figure 1.8

Customize your pen pressure and speed.

Meanwhile, Back at the Palettes

Just below the Brush Selector Bar is a set of palettes for choosing colors. The default color picker shown in Figure 1.9 has a hue (H) ring with a movable indicator (the tiny black circle) showing your color's position on the spectrum. The triangle inside the ring has another indicator (the tiny white circle) for saturation (S) and value (V), also called *brightness*. The little swatches at the lower-left corner show the current color is a rich magenta.

You might prefer to pick colors from an array of swatches called Color Sets. Figure 1.10 shows this palette open, along with a menu of choices for switching to a different color set or creating your own.

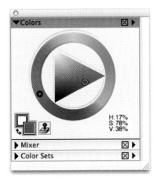

Figure 1.9

Pick a color, any color.

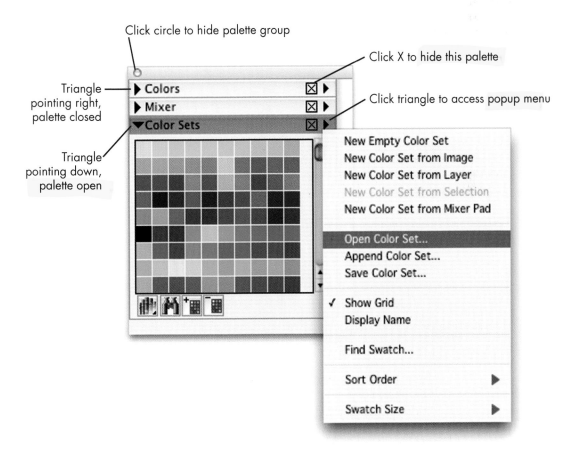

Click circle to hide palette group

Click X to hide this palette

Triangle pointing right, palette closed

Click triangle to access popup menu

Triangle pointing down, palette open

▶ Colors

▶ Mixer

▼Color Sets

New Empty Color Set
New Color Set from Image
New Color Set from Layer
New Color Set from Selection
New Color Set from Mixer Pad

Open Color Set...
Append Color Set...
Save Color Set...

✓ Show Grid
Display Name

Find Swatch...

Sort Order ▶

Swatch Size ▶

Figure 1.10

Switch to Color Sets swatches.

Little Triangles, Squares, and Circles

Most palettes have a popup menu of options, revealed when you click on the black triangle to the right of the palette name. The other black triangle, at the left edge, simply opens or closes the palette. You can hide a palette completely by clicking on the X on the right and hide a group of palettes by clicking the tiny circle at the upper left. You won't need the Layers Palette for this lesson, and you'll probably never need the Channels Palette, so make them go away now.

Pencils and Markers and Chalk—Oh My!

Dry media, such as pencils and chalk, respond to pressure changes with variation in opacity. Figure 1.11 shows marks made with Pencils > Grainy Pencil 5 and Chalk > Square Chalk 35. In real life, overlapping pencil or crayon strokes will build up, getting darker and denser. By contrast, chalk and pastels are opaque, so light colors can cover darker strokes. Notice that pink chalk strokes are able to cover up the darker brown underneath, but the same pink applied with a pencil gets even darker, almost red. Painter uses the terms *Cover* and *Buildup* to describe these two basic methods for determining the behavior of a brush variant. Do Felt Markers use the Cover or Buildup method? If you're not sure, or even if you are, test one of the variants in the Felt Pens category. Make overlapping strokes with any light color and see what happens.

Figure 1.11

Pencils and chalk.

We expect pencils and chalk to reveal the surface texture of the paper we are using, and digital dry media behaves as expected. I used three different paper textures, and the results are especially dramatic with the wide chalk marks. Lighter pressure reveals more of the paper surface because heavy strokes tend to fill in the depressions. Basic Paper has a subtle grain and is the default texture. Choose a different type of surface from the Paper Selector near the bottom of the Toolbox, or open the Papers Palette by selecting Window > Library Palettes > Show Papers. Figure 1.12 has the current paper library open to show thumbnail swatches.

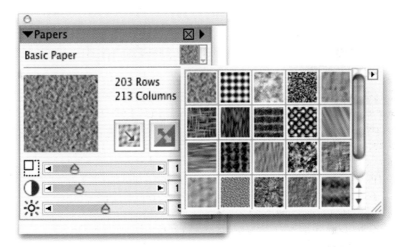

Figure 1.12

Pick your paper.

When Is Paper Not Paper?

When it's canvas or pavement or wood! Of course, you can draw and paint on a variety of surfaces that aren't paper. Painter uses the term generically, referring to any surface texture. The word "grainy" describes brush variants that can reveal texture, but "grainy" might not always be part of the variant's name.

Real Brushes (Almost)

Traditional brushes can have a variety of shapes and are composed of numerous bristles that can range in length, thickness, and stiffness. The kind of mark made by a brush depends on a large number of factors: quality and number of bristles, viscosity and amount of paint loaded, as well as pressure and direction of the artist's stroke. There are several categories devoted to bristle-type brushes. They include Oils, Acrylic, Impasto (Italian for "thick paint"), and new in Painter X, the intriguingly named RealBristle brushes. I made the orange and red strokes in Figure 1.13 with Oils > Bristle Oils 20 and used Artists' Oils > Dry Clumpy Impasto for the blue and purple strokes. Go ahead, try them. I'll wait here.

The Bristle Oils brush seems light and airy. It shows quite a lot of space between bristles along one edge, making for some lively effects when strokes overlap in different directions. The bristles of Dry Clumpy Impasto are more densely packed, and we see realistic striations in the thick paint. There is a smeary quality as well, so underlying color mixes with a new stroke. The trailing off of long strokes is not the result of reduced pen pressure—this brush actually runs out of paint!

Figure 1.13
Different strokes.

So Many Choices!

Every new version of Painter has more brush categories and variants than the previous version. I haven't actually multiplied the number of brush categories in Painter X by the number of variants in each category, but there's gotta be about a thousand to choose from. Just exploring a fraction of them and keeping track of the ones you like can be a challenge. Fortunately, every new version of the program also provides increasingly better ways to organize brushes and customize the workspace. Yes, you even have more choices for how to choose!

Keeping Track

Painter lets you find recently used and favorite brushes without having to search through all those lists in the Brush Selector Bar. Open the Tracker from the Window menu to see a list of the brush variants you've used so far. To return to a previous brush, simply click on its name in the Tracker. Figure 1.14 shows my Tracker after I finished making the scribble sampler.

Click on the black triangle to the right of the Tracker title bar to access some handy options. Brushes you want to use over and over can be locked, while others can be cleared from the list to keep it slim and trim.

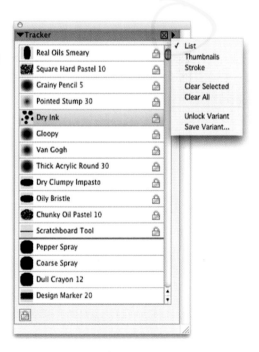

Figure 1.14
Automatic brush tracking.

Custom Palettes

After you've been working with Painter for a while, maybe tomorrow, you'll probably know what your favorite brushes, papers, and other art materials are. All of these can be combined in a compact little palette. Custom palettes are easy to make. Choose the brush variant you want and drag its icon away from the Brush Selector Bar. A new custom palette is created automatically, containing that brush. Add more brushes by simply dragging in more items. Hold the Shift key down to remove or reposition items. Figure 1.15 shows how I created a custom palette with most of my scribble brushes. I dragged a couple of paper textures in, too: Basic Paper and Artists Canvas.

Drag either the category icon or the variant icon to your canvas.

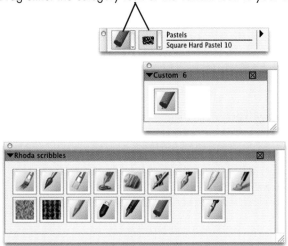

Figure 1.15

Make a custom palette.

Figure 1.16

Get organized.

Have It Your Way

Custom palettes are very versatile. You might want to have a different custom palette for sketching, painting, working with photos, or for a specific project. No problem. Manage them with the Custom Palette Organizer by selecting Window > Custom Palette > Organizer. Figure 1.16 shows my scribble palette highlighted and ready to be saved, using the Export command. It's available on the CD that accompanies this book. Load it now, using the Import command.

Back to the Drawing Board

Continue exploring more brushes, using the Rhoda Scribbles custom palette for help in making your selections. Here's a list of the brushes I used, in no special order, showing both category and variant (I'm leaving out the pixel sizes). As you sample each of them, see if you can match them to the strokes and squiggles I made. You don't need to imitate my scribbles, just identify them.

- Pens > Scratchboard Tool

- Pencils > Grainy Pencil

- Crayons > Dull Crayon

- Airbrushes > Coarse Spray (also, Graffiti)

- Calligraphy > Dry Ink

- Artists > Van Gogh

- Blenders > Pointed Stump

- Real Bristle Brushes > Real Oils Smeary (version X only)

- Oil Pastels > Chunky Oil Pastel

- Impasto > Gloopy

- Acrylics > Thick Acrylic Round

- Artists' Oils > Dry Clumpy Impasto

- Felt Pens > Design Marker

- Oils > Bristle Oils

Proceed at Your Own Risk!

You can explore other brush categories now or any time, but be warned—some of them are pretty wacky! For example, Pattern Pens don't apply the current color, but paint with the current pattern. (You'll find that library right under Papers at the bottom of the Toolbox.) Watercolor brushes require a special layer, created automatically when you use one of them. Then you have to switch back to the Canvas layer to use non-watercolor brushes. But Digital Watercolor variants can be applied directly to the canvas, needing no special layer. Liquid Ink is in a class (and layer) by itself. Well, you get the idea.

Control Yourself

Here are some exercises I recommend for developing skill with the Wacom tablet. Use them as a warm-up before you begin a work session and to check whether you need to re-set Preferences > Brush Tracking for your pressure and speed. Do the exercises in the order given. If you save them, you can observe your progress from one session to another.

Crosshatched Scribbles

Start with a new white canvas at least 6 inches square at 72 ppi. Choose Pens > Ball Point Pen 1.5 and use Black as the main color. Refer to Figure 1.17 as you work. For your first stroke make a rapid saw tooth vertical scribble that fills most of the canvas. You'll have better control if you support the side of your hand on the tablet and slide up and down. (Notice that the Ball Point Pen doesn't respond much to pressure changes, just like its real-world counterpart.) This first stroke should remind you of Bart Simpson needing a haircut. Your second stroke goes over the first, but it is horizontal. Then make each of the diagonal strokes on top of that. At this point your canvas should look like the lower-left corner of Figure 1.17.

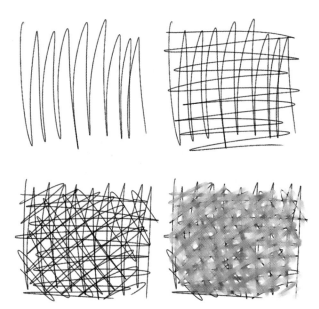

The Color formerly Known As...

Prior to Painter IX, "main color" was called "primary color" and "additional" color was called "secondary." This is a sensible change, because "primary" generally refers to the three pigment colors (red, blue, and yellow), and "secondary" colors refer to those resulting from mixing two primaries (orange, green, and purple).

Figure 1.17

Scribble and smear practice.

Now switch to a brush that smears without adding color by choosing Blenders > Grainy Water. Working on top of the same crosshatch scribble, repeat those four strokes again—vertical, horizontal, and two diagonals—for the result shown in the lower-right of Figure 1.17. That loosened you up, didn't it?

Practice Your Scales

Drawing is a lot like playing a musical instrument—ya gotta practice, practice, practice. With that comparison in mind, let's do some scales! Begin with a new canvas or simply eliminate your previous scribbles quickly with Select > All (Cmd/Ctrl+A) followed by pressing the Delete (Backspace) key.

This exercise will help you develop accurate placement of strokes. Let's use a pencil variant this time and a bright color. I used a Greasy Pencil to make rows of scales in Figure 1.18. Make a series of vertical scalloped curves, starting at either the top or the bottom. Working horizontally is okay, too. After a few rows, see if you can make an entire sequence of scales in one stroke. Switch direction (color, too) just for variety. If it's easier for you to work from left to right, try going the other way to challenge yourself. Fill up the canvas with scales of different sizes. I love that Greasy Pencil! With a little more practice, I bet I could work up a really good chain-link fence effect.

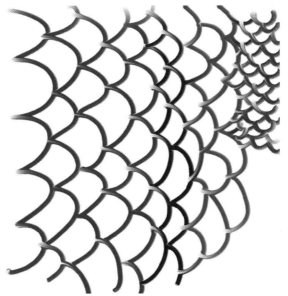

Figure 1.18

Nonmusical scales.

Pressure Control

Dry Ink is my favorite brush variant. One of the things I love about it is the extreme variation in stroke thickness as a function of pressure. You'll find it, for some strange reason, in the Calligraphy category. Clear your canvas once again, or start a new one. Make a long horizontal stroke that begins with light pen pressure and gradually increase pressure to the maximum as you end the stroke. My first practice stroke in Figure 1.19 shows an abrupt change in thickness, looking more like a corn dog than a tadpole. It might take several tries to get the right touch for a smooth transition. Alternate right-to-left strokes with left-to-right strokes, and try vertical strokes as well. Can you make a stroke that begins thin, swells to full width, and then tapers off?

Can You Handle the Pressure?

Making smooth transitions in line width is more challenging if you're working with a smaller tablet or models with fewer pressure levels (the Graphire series). If that's the case, it's especially important to tweak sensitivity of the tablet with Preferences > Brush Tracking.

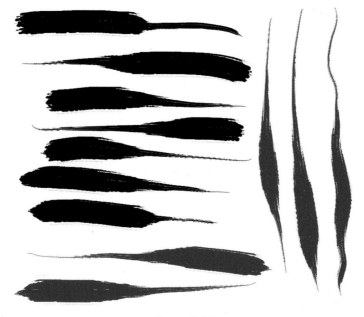

Figure 1.19

Dry Ink under pressure.

Make a Warm-Up Palette

Remember the custom palettes feature we explored earlier in this lesson? Refer to Figure 1.15 as a guide to making one for your warm-up brushes. The brushes I used for the exercises were as follows:

- Pens > Ball Point 1.5

- Blenders > Grainy Water

- Pencils > Greasy Pencil (any size)

- Calligraphy > Dry Ink

Is Dry Ink still your current brush? Drag its icon away from the Brush Selector to start a custom palette, then add each of the other three variants. If they aren't in the order you want, reposition an item by holding down the Shift key as you drag it. The Shift key allows you to remove items, also. Give your new custom palette a descriptive name with the Custom Palette Organizer. Figure 1.20 shows the Palette Name dialog box, which appears when you click on the Rename button. You can type in any name you like.

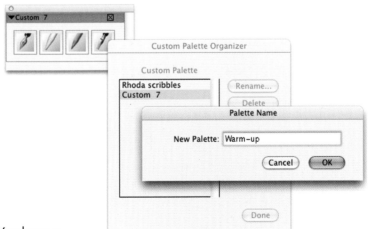

Figure 1.20

Rename the palette.

What's Next?

You're off to a good start. You have a basic understanding of how to choose and organize Painter brushes and how to show your Wacom tablet who's boss. In the following lessons, you'll practice skills and learn the concepts for improving your mastery of drawing and painting. I promise to take you way beyond scribbling.

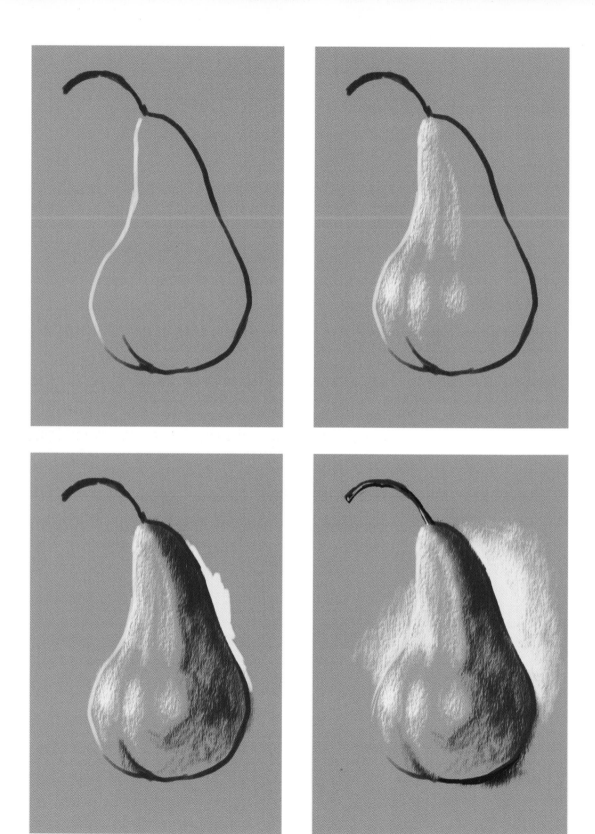

2 Basic Drawing

In this lesson, we'll start with a simple subject and practice drawing it using several methods. Painter offers beginners some "training wheels." Use them as long as you want. When you're feeling less wobbly, simply take them off and draw freely.

The Pear

Open Pear.jpg from the source image folder on the CD that accompanies this book (see Figure 2.1). It's a good example of a simple still life subject. It looks good enough to eat *and* draw (not necessarily in that order). There are other delicious images in the Produce section of the folder. All are ripe for the picking and painting.

Size Matters

You may want to change the size of the pear image to fit your screen. That's easy. Selecting Canvas > Resize brings up the Resize dialog box, shown in Figure 2.2. Before you enter the new height or width, be sure to uncheck the Constrain File Size box. If you don't, the change in dimensions will be compensated with a change in resolution, and the image will be exactly the same size on screen!

Figure 2.1

A classic subject.

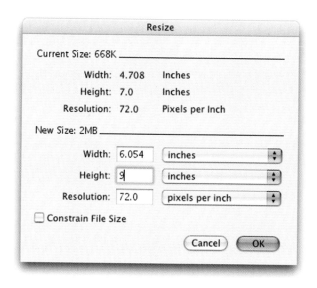

Figure 2.2

Don't constrain file size.

Clone-and-Trace

Take a good look at the pear. Ignore the bruises and scratches, and focus on the edges of the shape. It is made up of a series of curves. The easiest way to make a simple outline of this shape is to trace it, and the easiest way to set up Painter's Tracing Paper function is to click File > Quick Clone. Painter automatically creates an exact copy of the image, names it Clone of pear.jpg, deletes the image to give you a blank canvas, and shows you the original pear at 50% opacity (see Figure 2.3). You'll need to keep the original (Clone Source) open while you work on the clone. Figure 2.3 points out the icon that toggles tracing paper on or off (keyboard shortcut is Cmd/Ctrl+T), which you'll need to do as your sketch develops.

Tracing Paper toggle

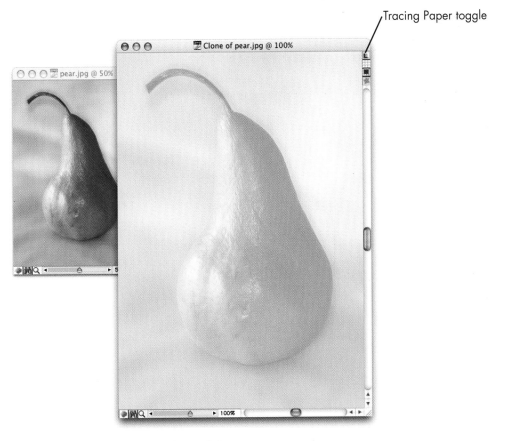

Figure 2.3

Tracing Paper at 50% opacity.

Opacity Capacity

Painter X introduces changeable opacity for tracing paper. Just hold down the tracing paper icon to choose thicker or thinner paper. This is a handy feature for accommodating different stages in your drawing or different kinds of source images.

So, you just need to pick a brush variant and a color, and you're ready to trace. I chose a rich brown, sampled from the shadow side of the pear source image. You don't have to actually switch to the Eyedropper tool to pick a color from an open image—just hold down the Opt/Alt key and your brush cursor becomes an eyedropper. After you click on the color you want, release the modifier key and it's a Brush tool again.

Use a Crayon, Pencil, or Colored Pencil variant for lines that show paper grain. My simple sketch in Figure 2.4 was done with Sharp Colored Pencil 7. I started with the stem, using heavy pressure and several strokes to add thickness. It took three curved strokes to draw the right side of the fruit, and then I overlapped a couple of strokes to emphasize weight at the bottom of the shape. A hint of the pear's "cleavage" was made with very light pressure. Don't forget to turn off Tracing Paper to see your drawing!

Dude! Where's My Clone Source?

If you accidentally close the source image while you're working, or if the relationship between the source and the clone is "broken" for any reason, reconnecting them is easy. Open the source image again and select File > Clone Source to designate it as the one you want for reference.

Figure 2.4
Pear-shaped sketch.

Tonal Drawing

This outline drawing looks flat. Examine the pear photo again, and this time notice the areas of light and shadow. We'll do another drawing that emphasizes these light and dark shapes, so we can create the illusion of depth. A traditional way to render light and dark effectively involves working on medium gray or tinted paper. Paper color does a lot of the work, and all you have to do is add the lightest and darkest parts.

Save your outline drawing, if you wish, and use the Quick Clone command for a fresh canvas. Sample a medium to light orange color from the left side of the fruit, but not the brightest part. Choose Set Paper Color from the Canvas menu. Nothing happened yet, but when you choose Select > All (Cmd/Ctrl+A) and Delete/Backspace, your new color will fill the blank canvas. (Painter defines Paper Color as the color revealed by an Eraser. So, you just erased the whole image.)

This time I'm using a Conte stick for the outline, but I switched to white for the left edge, indicating the light source. Real French Conte sticks are firmer and creamier than chalk or charcoal, and Painter creates the illusion digitally quite well. Figure 2.5 was done with Tapered Conte 8. That white line implies volume, like an embossed shape raised a bit from the paper surface.

Little Triangles, Squares, and Circles

Most palettes have a popup menu of options, revealed when you click on the black triangle to the right of the palette name. The other black triangle, at the left edge, simply opens or closes the palette. You can hide a palette completely by clicking on the X on the right and hide a group of palettes by clicking the tiny circle at the upper left. You won't need the Layers palette for this lesson, and you'll probably never need the Channels palette, so make them go away now.

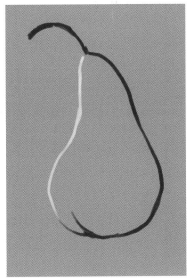

Figure 2.5
A hint of depth.

Serial Save

A great feature in versions IX and X is Iterative Save in the File menu. When you want to save stages in the development of an image, this command automatically numbers each version in order. File format must be RIFF, Painter's default format. Use it for this project, and any project—you'll thank me someday.

Take another close look at the pear and notice its texture, most apparent where the light shines obliquely but not directly on the fruit. To bring out that texture, we will use a strongly "grainy" variant, such as Pastels > Round Hard Pastels. First, choose a paper texture that imitates the pear's skin. It's not always easy to predict what a texture will look like just from the paper swatches, even when they are displayed as thumbnails. Figure 2.6 shows not only the swatches of the current Paper library but also sliders to control size, brightness, and contrast adjustments.

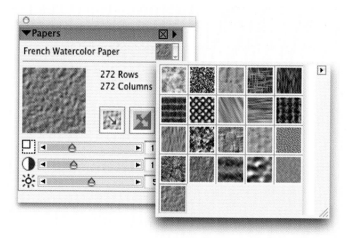

Figure 2.6
Show us your swatches!

Go ahead and test a few textures on a new canvas the same orange color as your pear drawing, using white with a Hard Pastel variant. The top row of Figure 2.7 shows three papers that won't work for this project: Pebble Board, Hard Laid Paper, and Coarse Cotton Canvas. Any of the bottom three papers will do nicely. They are, from left to right, Italian Watercolor, Rough Charcoal, and Charcoal Paper. With slightly vertical striations, Charcoal Paper is just about perfect. There is a custom palette for this project in the Palettes and Libraries folder on the CD, called Tonal Pear. It includes the paper swatch. Import it to your workspace with the Custom Palette Organizer.

Now that you have the outline, you don't really need tracing paper anymore, so turn it off and use the "eyeball" method—just look at the source photo to guide your placement of highlights and shadows. Apply a few white strokes with a Hard Pastel variant in the light areas, pressing harder in the brightest spots. Sample the dark brown color from the outline to create the shadow areas. Try not to let white and brown strokes overlap or even touch each other, but rely on the paper color to express mid-tones. Only a few strokes are needed to bring out this voluptuous form. Refer to Figure 2.8 for guidance and encouragement.

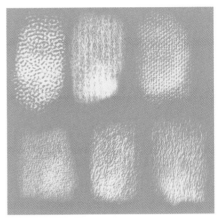

Figure 2.7
Papers, please!

Figure 2.8
Easy does it—let the paper show through.

Switch to the Conte stick to make a clean white edge where the light background meets the darkest part of the pear. Go back to Hard Pastel to add some white background on both sides of the pear, feathering out the edges with light pressure.

Figure 2.9 shows my completed drawing, with a few finishing touches. I added a small cast shadow under the pear. A couple of details on the stem were made with Charcoal > Sharp Charcoal Pencil 5, drawn in white and with the paper color. Finally, I gently removed some of the white outline on the lower left of the pear, allowing it to merge into the background. No need to switch to an Eraser variant for those last few strokes—use the other end of your Wacom pen!

Figure 2.9
A nice piece of fruit.

Are We There Yet?

How do you know when you're finished with a drawing or painting? If you've spent more than 15 minutes on this one, you're done! Trying to make your artwork perfect? Fuhgeddaboudit!

Crosshatch Contours

Take yet another close look at the pear. This time, concentrate on its rounded contours. We'll work on white paper with black lines. Tone and form will be built up from overlapping strokes that follow the contours of the pear. This is another traditional method often used by cartoonists and graphic artists, especially for commercial black-and-white printing.

So, make another Quick Clone of the photo. Choose a thin pencil or pen that has little or no variation in thickness or opacity. I'm using the 2B Pencil. Sketch the stem and right edge of the pear quickly and begin to make a series of roughly parallel strokes that follow the curves of the fruit. Use strokes that vary in length and direction, building up the form. Your wrist will have to twist as you work.

For darker areas, overlap strokes in different directions. This is similar to the warm-up crosshatch exercise you did in Lesson 1—just a bit more controlled. Figure 2.10 shows the process, and the result can be very lively.

Figure 2.10
Are we pear, yet?

Don't Hurt Yourself

To keep from twisting your wrist too much, use Painter's cool Rotate Page tool, available in all versions. It shares a space on the Toolbox with the Grabber hand, right next to the Magnifier. Figure 2.11 shows the tool active and the image tilted as desired. When you're ready to return to normal orientation, double-click the Rotate Page tool.

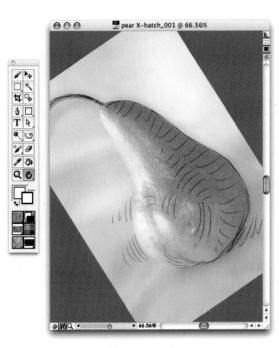

Figure 2.11
Let's do the twist!

Send In the Clones

If you've completed all the drawing exercises in this lesson, you've earned a treat. I don't mean eating the pear—but it was delicious (tossed with lettuce, celery, walnuts, and bleu cheese dressing). No, I'm referring to Painter's incredible feature for turning photos into drawings and paintings, not by clicking on filter effects, but created one brush stroke at a time! And, yes, you're the one applying the brush strokes.

Taking Responsibility

Actually, you can get Painter to do all the work while you take a coffee break. Check out Painter X's new Smart Stroke Brush category, used in conjunction with the new Auto-Painting Palette. But that's not art, just a parlor trick. I use Painter to help me prepare an image and provide some shortcuts, but I reserve the right to make each stroke myself. Yes, that's where I really draw the line!

We've been using only the Tracing Paper feature of cloning so far. You can turn any variant into a Cloner Brush by enabling the Clone Color check box on the color picker. Its icon is a rubber stamp. Figure 2.12 shows Clone Color on, with the usual color selection area faded to indicate it's not available. For the current brush variant, then, all color information will be coming from the Clone Source: hue, saturation, and value (brightness). You'll see how this works in a minute.

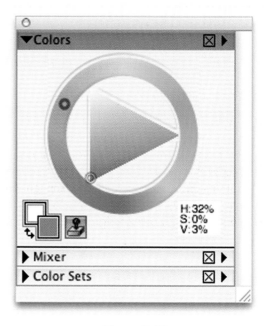

Figure 2.12
Color info will come from the Clone Source.

Let's make a clone drawing. Open the pear image again, and use the Quick Clone command. Choose Pastels > Square Hard Pastels 10 and the Charcoal Paper texture used earlier. Enable Clone Color and apply strokes following the contour of the pear (that's generally a good practice whatever medium you use). Make Tracing Paper more opaque as you go so you can see your work. Include a few strokes under the pear and in the background. Does your drawing look something like Figure 2.13? How cool is that?

Where Are the Clones?

Cloner brushes have always been the most exciting feature of Painter, in my not so humble opinion. There are 38 brush styles to choose from. Version X provides a handy way to jump to the Cloner category instantly. Choose the Cloner tool in the Toolbox. (Look for the brush icon with a little cross-hair indicating a clone source.) Its roommate is the Rubber Stamp tool, used for point-to-point cloning: with your Option/Alt key engaged, click on the pixel area you want as the source. Release the modifier key, and you can paint from that source to anywhere else on the image.

Figure 2.13
Pastel clone drawing.

Pick a Pepper

How about making a chalk/pastel drawing of something other than the pear? If you'd like a change of pace, open one of the chili pepper photos from the Produce section of the source images on the CD. This pepper has such a fascinating shape that I took several shots of different "poses," some in bright sunlight and some indoors on a semi-gloss gray background—my Wacom tablet. Let's work with ChiliSunlit1.jpg, shown in Figure 2.14.

Figure 2.14

This is not a pear.

Painter X introduces a way to prepare an image to enhance the effectiveness of cloning, based on the type of clone you plan to make. These choices are found in the new Underpainting Palette (found under Window > Show Underpainting), shown in Figure 2.15. I chose a new color scheme optimized for chalk drawing. The result, in Figure 2.16, is a less saturated, warmer tonality. Make a Quick Clone of this version, and then select File > Save As to choose the RIFF file format. Now you can preserve the stages of your drawing with Iterative Save.

Figure 2.15

The Underpainting Palette.

Figure 2.16

Prepared pepper.

This time you'll use an approach I call "scribble, smear, and pick." There is a custom palette for this technique in the Palettes and Libraries folder on the CD. It includes my choice of texture, Sandy Pastel Paper. Import it now, or you can select the same variants I'm using:

- Pastels > Tapered Pastel 10

- Blenders > Pointed Stump 10

- Chalk > Sharp Chalk

Begin with the Tapered Pastel, using Clone Color. Make rough scribbles over most of the pepper, guided by the contours of the shape. Include the cast shadow and some of the background. The top image in Figure 2.17 shows this stage. Switch to the Blender and smooth out some (not all) of your scribbled strokes. Look closely at this stage with Tracing Paper turned off, comparing it to the source image. Decide which details you want to bring out. Pick out those details with Sharp Chalk, using Clone Color.

The final stage shows more detail on the stem and the small highlight on the upper part of the pepper near the stem. One very subtle but important element is the thin rim of reflection between the core shadow on the lower right of the pepper and the cast shadow. This could not be made with Clone Color, so I disabled that option, selected a light color, and drew it in with Sharp Chalk.

Figure 2.17
Scribble, smear, and pick.

Repetitive Pepper

Prepare to make a pencil clone of the pepper. Go back to the original bright color scheme and use a Grainy Cover Pencil variant with Clone Color enabled. Change brush size as needed. Try a technique similar to the crosshatch contours you used on the pear (refer to Figure 2.10), allowing quite a bit of white paper to show through. Start with a quick outline of all the shapes, including the shadows.

Quick-Change Artist

To change only the size of your brush, it's not necessary to choose another variant. Just use the bracket keys: the left bracket ([) makes the brush smaller, the right bracket (]) makes it larger. This is especially handy when cloning because you must enable Clone Color every time you switch to a different variant.

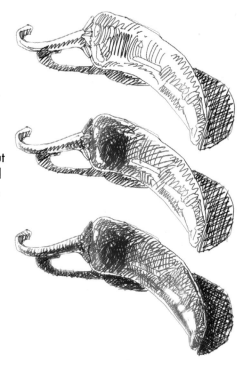

Figure 2.18 shows the development of my pencil clone sketch. Notice the outlines around highlight shapes in the early stage. Playful scribbles are mixed with crosshatching, building up tone in the shadows and darker parts of the pepper. Your sketch will have its own style and character—and spicy flavor.

I'll return to cloning techniques in future lessons, but I just couldn't wait to introduce you to this powerful feature. No offense to the fabulous folks at Adobe, but Painter's Cloner brushes leave Photoshop in the dust!

Figure 2.18
Hot and spicy.

What's Next?

Keep practicing your tonal drawing and crosshatch techniques, with or without the aid of Clone Color. There are source photos on the CD that came with this book to serve as subjects for drawing and painting at every skill level. I also encourage you to go to the market and buy some nice fresh produce to work with. Make your own photos, but even better, set your hand-picked fruit or vegetable on a surface next to your computer and draw it live! Aim a spotlight on one side to get dramatic highlights and shadows. Figure 2.19 shows a basic setup.

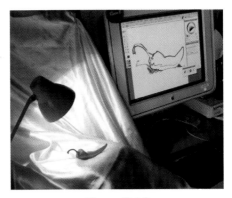

Figure 2.19
Chili pepper LIVE.

After every lesson or practice session, choose your best couple of drawings, or a series showing three or four stages in its development, and print them. That way you'll have tangible evidence of your work to hang on the walls. Over time, you'll be able to observe how your skills improve. Examining a print of your drawing is also a good way to evaluate it for possible changes.

Most desktop inkjet printers can create very high-quality output. To enhance the fine art nature of your image, use special paper or other media designed for your printer. High-gloss heavy-weight photo paper might be ideal for some projects, and canvas or watercolor paper might be better for others. I printed my pencil clone pepper series on glossy photo paper for crisp lines and intense color. The chalk cloned peppers (from Figure 2.17) are softer and more painterly, so I printed that series on a Canvas sheet. See the Appendix for resources.

Drawing or Painting?

What's the difference? Sometimes not much, and we may use these terms interchangeably. In general, drawings are made with dry media, paintings with wet. Or, if you render your subject mostly with lines, it's a drawing. But when tones and colors blend into each other without distinct edges, it's a painting. So when you smeared the chalk lines on your pepper clone with a Blender variant, did your drawing change into a painting? I'll let you decide. A traditional term for artwork composed with a variety of wet and dry materials, possibly incorporating photos or collage elements pasted on, is *mixed media*. We'll be doing a lot of that.

Technically, everything you make in Painter is *painting* because it's done with pixels. Digital "drawing" requires a vector-based program like Illustrator. I'm glad I could clear that up.

3 Working with Layers

Regardless of subject matter or style, it's often a good idea to separate elements of your art work into layers. For example, draw outlines on one layer and create color on another. You'll be able to make changes to either layer while protecting the other.

The Chair

You'll see how layers work with a simple drawing of a chair. We'll use the one shown in Figure 3.1.

Open the file beige_armchair.jpg, found in Things > Furniture on the CD that accompanies this book. Use Canvas > Resize if needed to fit the image on your screen. Make a Quick Clone to access the Tracing Paper feature. Choose a pen variant that has some thick-and-thin response to pressure on your tablet but no variation in opacity. I suggest either the Scratchboard Tool or Croquil Pen 5.

Working with black, make a loose sketch of the chair's basic shapes, similar to Figure 3.2. Use heavier pressure to create stronger lines, such as on the outer edge of the chair's shape, and a lighter touch for inside shapes and creases. Ignore shading and texture for now—we'll use additional layers for that. Also ignore the shadow under the chair, the table next to it, and (very important) the price tag!

Figure 3.1
Pull up a chair.

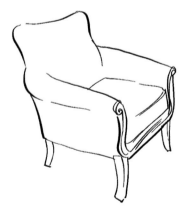

Figure 3.2
Have a seat.

Adjust Visibility

It will be easier to see the clone source (chair photo) with the opacity of your drawing turned down to about 30 percent. Painter X allows you to do that by holding down the tracing paper icon at the top-right edge of your image window. (Figure 3.3 points it out, as well as another item you'll use later in the lesson.) You'll be able to see your work just fine because you're using black lines instead of subtle painted strokes.

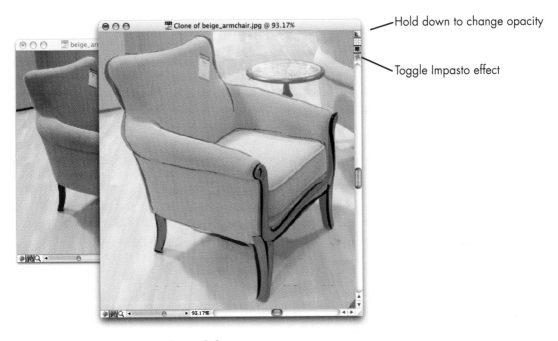

Hold down to change opacity

Toggle Impasto effect

Figure 3.3
Takes two to toggle.

Add a Color Layer

You'll make a new layer for color. If you don't see the Layers Palette on your workspace, launch it from the Window menu. Figure 3.4 shows where to click to create a new layer and where to change the composite method for determining how the layer will interact with the Canvas image (or with other layers).

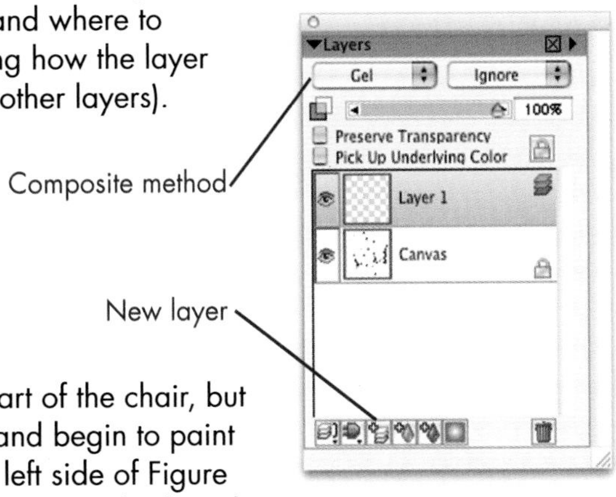

Composite method

New layer

Figure 3.4
Have another layer.

Sample a peachy beige color from a light part of the chair, but not the brightest. Choose Pens > Flat Color and begin to paint on the new layer. If your work looks like the left side of Figure 3.5, your layer is still using the default composite method, and it is covering up your line drawing. To change that, switch to either Gel or Multiply.

Figure 3.5
Composite method matters.

The Flat Color variant is too big for this project, so reduce its size with the Size slider in the Property Bar at the top of your workspace. Are you able to see a "ghost" image of the brush size when your Wacom pen hovers over the image? If not, you might want to choose Enable Brush Ghosting in Preferences > General menu.

Speed versus Visibility

Brush Ghosting gives useful visual cues about your current brush, but there can be a downside to that. If you're using a complex brush, such as a RealBristle variant, and your computer is older or less powerful than the latest models, the result is slower brush action. When that happens, just turn off Brush Ghosting.

Paint flat color over the chair, without being too careful about staying within the lines. The deliberately imperfect application of color in Figure 3.6 looks fine. Use a darker mahogany color for the wood. Should I remind you to use Iterative Save for this project? (I'm such a nag!)

Figure 3.6
Flat finish.

Add Tone and Texture

Create an additional layer, this one for the lights and shadows, as well as a bit of texture. We'll use a Grainy variant this time to reveal paper grain. First, make a custom paper using the fabric on the chair.

Make a New Paper

Zoom in on the chair photo so you can see the parquet-like pattern in the fabric. Make a rectangular selection on an area with no variation in lighting. (The Rectangular Selection tool is just under the Brush tool in the Toolbox.) Select Edit > Copy (Cmd/Ctrl+C) followed by Edit > Paste in New Image so that you have this fabric swatch in its own document. Now enlarge the pattern so it will show up better on the drawing: use Canvas > Resize and double either the width or height. (Remember to uncheck Constrain File Size.) Papers are simply repeating grayscale "tiles," so let's eliminate color. Painter X offers Desaturate as a choice in the Photo Enhance options on the Underpainting Palette. (For earlier versions, select Effects > Tonal Control > Adjust Colors and drag the Saturation slider all the way to the left.) Click on Apply, then increase contrast as well for a bolder pattern.

OK, you're ready to turn this swatch into a new paper. Choose Select > All (Cmd/Ctrl+A) and then choose Capture Paper from the popup menu on the Papers Palette. Give it a name, as shown in Figure 3.7, and this new paper automatically joins the others in your current library.

With Parquet Weave (or whatever you called it) as your active paper, use a hard Chalk or Pastel variant to stroke in some darker and lighter areas on the new layer. Don't rely on Clone Color this time, but choose color with the Option/Alt shortcut to the Eyedropper while your Brush tool is active. A great way to see all the available colors in an image is to create a color set from the image. Find Color Sets as part of the Colors Palette group. With the original armchair photo active, choose New Color Set From Image in the Color Sets popup menu. You'll see something like Figure 3.8.

Figure 3.7
Paper trail.

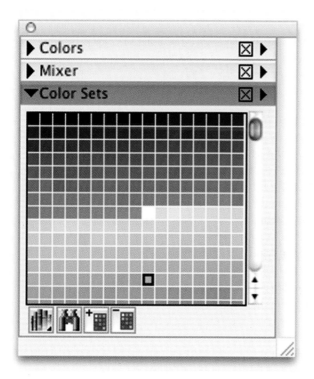

Figure 3.8
Chair colors.

The textured and toned chair is shown in Figure 3.9. The layered stages were saved automatically in RIFF format. To flatten your composite and save it as a JPEG or in another file format, use the Drop All command in the Layers popup menu.

Figure 3.9
Chair in three layers.

Organize Your Papers

Those six little swatches at the bottom of the Toolbox show art materials that are organized in libraries. You can swap to other collections with the Open Library command, and you can organize your own libraries with the Mover utility available for each resource.

Make a custom Paper library. Choose Paper Mover from the popup menu on the Papers Palette. The Paper Mover dialog box opens with thumbnail swatches of all the items in the default Painter Papers library displayed on the left. There is an empty area on the right. To start a new collection, click the New button and give your library a name. Now you can drag items you like from the default collection to your new one. Don't forget to include your upholstery pattern from the chair exercise. Figure 3.10 has some of my favorite papers dragged over to my new custom library. I can add items from other libraries by using the Open and Close commands on the left side. (You must close a library before you can open another one. Then the Close button changes to the Open button.)

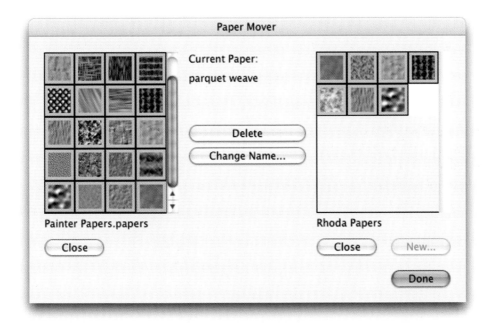

Figure 3.10
Get your papers in order.

Papers, Please!

You'll find exciting paper collections provided by Corel with your current Painter program or from previous versions, as well as a few on the CD that comes with this book. I love some of the default papers from Painter 7, so I've added them to my library of favorites. It's so easy to make new paper textures, you'll be creating your own for special projects or just for fun. A scan or photo of repeating items or random scatters of small objects can make great paper textures. Coffee beans, M&Ms, paper clips, fallen leaves, tire tracks—somebody stop me!

More Furniture

You'll create a painting from a photo of the leather loveseat in Figure 3.11. It's hard to believe the playful and colorful image at the beginning of this lesson started out as this understated classic. Layers will be used in several ways for this project, as well as cloning, smearing, scribbling, and—well, I don't want to give away all the details.

Figure 3.11
Classic seating.

Scheming and Smearing

With a lively color palette in mind, let's take advantage of the Color Scheme menu in the Underpainting Palette provided in Painter X. I chose the Chalk Drawing Scheme for one of the chili pepper drawings in Lesson 2. This time, use Impressionist Scheme for the dramatic effect in Figure 3.12. Also shown in Figure 3.12 is the color set made from the new image. I saved this color set as Loveseat.colors, and it's available in the custom palettes and libraries folder on the CD. It can be useful to guide your color choices if you're using an earlier version of Painter.

Figure 3.12
Colorful setting for seating.

Use File > Clone to make a copy of the image. Don't use Quick Clone this time because we don't want the copy deleted. Work on the clone copy with a smeary variant from the Blenders category to wipe out details and create a painterly background. Have some fun experimenting with several Blender brushes. Strokes made by some of them are slow on less powerful computers, even when Brush Ghosting is turned off in Preferences. If you're in a hurry, use Grainy Water or a Pointed Stump. I used Pointed Stump 30, mostly, for the result in Figure 3.13.

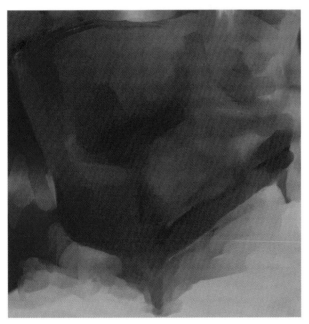

Figure 3.13
Smudged, smeary, and blurred.

Can You Unsmear?

Did your smearing go too far? Recover some of the original detail where needed by using Cloners > Soft Cloner to paint back details to be smeared again.

A Clone Painting Layer

Make a new layer, leaving your smeary version protected on the canvas. For this stage, you'll use Cloner variants or other brushes with Clone Color enabled to bring out the details impressionistically. There actually is an Impressionist Cloner you can use on this layer if you wish, but try some other brush styles as well.

I'm dying to try out the new RealBristle brushes in Painter X, so I'll start with those. Turn Tracing Paper up to high opacity, around 70 percent, so you see just enough of the original photo to place highlights and shadows. Using Clone Color, paint in some strokes on the lightest and darkest areas, following the contour of shapes for the direction of your brush. Figure 3.14 shows the development of the painting after applying some strokes with the Real Tapered Flat and Real Flat Opaque variants. Figure 3.15 shows only the new layer, so you can see how relatively few strokes were needed.

You may want to see how the smeary version on the canvas looks without the new layer. Just toggle visibility of any layer (or the canvas itself) with the eyeball icons in the Layers Palette.

Figure 3.14
Details emerging.

Figure 3.15
Canvas invisible.

An Impasto Layer

Let's add another layer for some thick paint strokes. The Impasto category offers a wide range of choices, and there are a few Impasto variants lurking in other categories for you to discover. You'll try them on the new layer, leaving the previous layer and the canvas untouched. This time, I'll pick colors from the custom color set, rather than use Clone Color. Work freely, with the confidence that anything you do can be undone, redone, or faded.

My Impasto layer, shown in Figure 3.16, was made with different sizes of the Thick Tapered Flat variant. The Layers Palette at this stage is also shown. I gave layers descriptive names (to replace the generic Layer 1, etc.) using Layer Attributes, available in the Layers popup menu or just by double-clicking a layer in the palette.

fading fast

Don't rush to undo a stroke you like just because it's too bright or too opaque. Use Edit > Fade to tone it down by any percentage you choose. And since I'm already warning you, be sure to have your image displayed at 100 percent when working with Impasto effects. At lower magnification, you'll see crazy moire patterns that really aren't there.

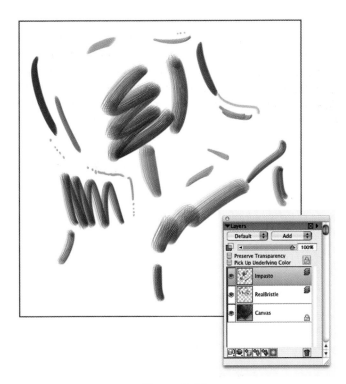

Figure 3.16
Thick paint.

Figure 3.17 shows my composite at this point. Before moving forward, there are some choices to consider:

- Erase parts of a layer
- Reduce a layer's opacity
- Change the composite method of a layer
- Alter the Impasto depth effect
- Add another layer

I ended up using all of those options before finishing up with the art work at the beginning of this lesson.

Out of Our Depth

The Impasto strokes are exciting, but they overpower the rest of the painting. Toggle depth on or off with the vaguely star-shaped icon on the right edge of the image window (refer back to Figure 3.3 if necessary) to see what your Impasto strokes look like when they are completely flat. How to achieve a reduction, but not elimination of paint depth? I reduced the opacity of the Impasto layer using the slider near the top of the Layers Palette. This resulted in less color but no change in the depth effect. Hmm, so it's not going to be that easy. It's important to know that for the Impasto category of brushes, color and depth are independent of each other. There are several Impasto variants for managing depth while leaving color alone. I chose the Depth Equalizer (sounds like something you'd need on a submarine) and gently stroked over some of the thick paint to make it a bit more subtle. Mission accomplished.

Figure 3.17
Not quite finished.

Everything's Under Control

Next time you use an Impasto variant, try a few strokes with opacity adjusted in the Property Bar. Figure 3.18 shows a test of the Thick Tapered Flat variant at 100%, 50%, and 30% opacity, using about the same stylus pressure.

Notice the other controls on the Property Bar. They are context sensitive, changing to show options for the tool you currently have selected in the Toolbox and also changing to accommodate the specific brush category you're using. Size and opacity don't need to be explained, but some of the other controls are not so obvious. The Grain setting is available for variants that show paper texture. A lower setting produces a stronger texture. This seems counterintuitive until you understand that lower values reduce penetration into the grain, while higher values increase penetration. Complete penetration (100% Grain) is no texture at all!

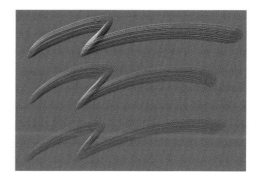

Figure 3.18
Testing your depth.

Resat means resaturation and refers to the amount of color replenished in the stroke. Blender variants do not add color at all but only smear existing color, so they have a Resat setting of zero. Bleed refers to the amount of mixing with underlying color, so you can expect Blenders to have relatively high values for Bleed. Open a photo or any image and try changing one or more control variables to see how smeary strokes are affected by changes in Resat and Bleed. Or make a new blank canvas to check out changes to other kinds of brushes.

Default Lies Not in Our Stars...

All changes you make to a variant will remain until you deliberately restore the default settings, using the aptly named Restore Default Variant command in the Brush Selector Bar popup menu. If you tweak a bunch of controls and come up with a really great custom brush that you don't want to lose, play it safe and use the Save Variant command, giving your special brush a unique name. It will take its place alphabetically in the current brush category.

Finishing Touches

Now I can admit that I had no clear idea where I was headed with this loveseat piece. So I'm not at all sure when it's done. Actually, this is just the kind of adventure I enjoy—plunging into unknown territory with very little chance of physical injury!

The third and last layer, a quick line sketch made with the other layers' visibility turned off to minimize distractions, was drawn with the Croquil 5 Pen in a dark blue-green from the color set. That layer stands alone in Figure 3.19.

Those few lines, so casually drawn, tie the image together. It turned out not to be an impressionist painting as traditionally defined, and that's okay. Before dropping all the layers, I switched the composite method for the line layer, with a couple of interesting variations competing for final honors. The two versions in Figure 3.20 show the Difference and Reverse Out methods for the line layer. Notice that Impasto depth is turned off.

Figure 3.19

Relyin' on the line.

Figure 3.20

Two runners up.

Here's how to add a colorful border. Be sure the canvas is highlighted, not a layer. Selecting Canvas > Canvas Size gives you fields to enter the number of extra pixels you need in any direction. Enter the same number of pixels for top, bottom, left, and right to get an even border. Then find the color you want and use the Paint Bucket tool to fill the new pixels.

Show Us Your Edges

The Underpainting Palette in Painter X has a great group of features. In addition to the Color Scheme and Photo Enhance choices, it also provides vignette Edge Effects for fading out the edges of your photo source.

What's Next?

You've had a taste of layers, enough to demonstrate that they can provide more than just an alternative to saving successive versions in the development of a painting. You also got to nibble the edges of Brush Controls. There are many more variables influencing brush behavior (and flavor) than you see on the Property Bar, enough to satiate any control freak, and more than enough to give the rest of us—well, a tummy ache.

When you use Window > Brush Controls > Show General, you'll open the Brush Controls Palette shown in Figure 3.21. It is actually a large group of palettes, with sections that are more or less useful, depending on the category of brush you're working with. You might never use some of these sections, and you certainly won't need to have more than a few showing at one time. Customize any palette group by closing the sections you don't need: just click the X in the upper-right corner.

When you have a sense of which palettes you want access to, place them exactly the way you want them and hide the rest. Use Window > Arrange Palettes > Save Layout to name this layout for easy access. Have different palette layouts for special projects, one for sketching, another for clone painting from a photo, and so on.

Painter X lets you customize every aspect of the program and save them all as a workspace. Yes, you can have several workspace arrangements for different projects or techniques. You can export a workspace to another hard drive or import the workspaces of other users. There are some that came with your Painter X program discs. If you want to see how John Derry works (he's one of the original creators of Painter) or look over the freckled shoulder of Cher Threinen-Pendarvis (author of the Painter WOW! series), import their workspaces. It might not make you more creative, but it couldn't hurt.

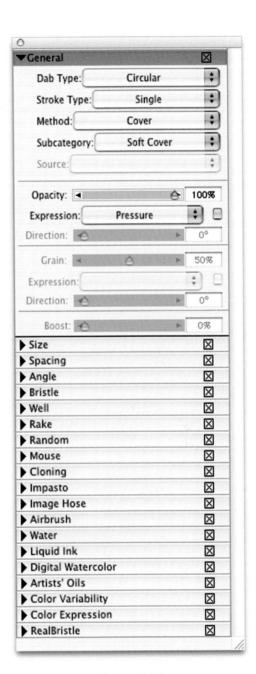

Figure 3.21
I got your Brush Controls right here!

4 The Great Outdoors

So far we've worked with single objects, food, and furniture. Let's take on more complex subject matter, such as landscapes and street scenes. No need to actually be exposed to the elements or the prying eyes (and harsh criticism) of tourists. We'll work from photographs. Later on, though, you're encouraged to pack your lunch with your laptop and set out for digital *Plein Aire* painting in the park.

Landscape

Open the file 5_trees.jpg, shown in Figure 4.1 and found in the Lesson 4 folder on the CD. Let's look closely at it to plan our strategy.

The Big Picture

The first thing to do with a complex subject—simplify it. Traditional artists have a great low-tech way to reduce detail and just see a composition of light and shadow. It's called *squinting*. When you do that, you'll see past the individual branches and notice that the entire upper half of the image is mostly dark, with just a few patches of light as "negative shapes." The bottom one-third is, basically, a mid-tone that visually anchors the strong vertical dark shapes. For me, the most intriguing areas are the very bright negative shapes between the tree trunks. They also make a bold horizontal band in contrast with the dark vertical shapes.

Figure 4.1

Trees a crowd.

Combining some techniques used in earlier lessons, you'll paint both with and without Clone Color, and we'll use tinted paper. The first stage in your painting will simplify shapes and minimize detail. Later, you'll add selected details, like a few bits of sky showing through tree branches and patches of sunlight on the grass.

Color Settings

Before you start painting, let's try a new color scheme from the Underpainting Palette (found in the Window > Underpainting menu). I like the Classical color scheme, shown in Figure 4.2. That chocolate brown looks yummy, and there is now less detail in the branches, an unexpected benefit. This image is provided in the Lesson 4 folder as 5_trees_ClassicalCS.jpg, for users of Painter IX or earlier.

Choose New Color Set from Image in the Color Sets popup menu. It will be useful sooner or later, probably both. This new color set, shown in Figure 4.3, might look a bit different from yours. I chose a slightly larger swatch size: 8 x 16 pixels. I also changed the sort order to LHS so that the swatches are arranged primarily according to Lightness (L). You can choose to have them sorted by Hue (H) or Saturation (S), whichever makes more visual sense to you.

Figure 4.2

Classical trees.

Get Set

It's quick and easy to make a new color set from the current image. I suggest doing it routinely as part of your basic preparation for painting with a photo. You'll have it handy whenever you need to choose a color in harmony with the source image.

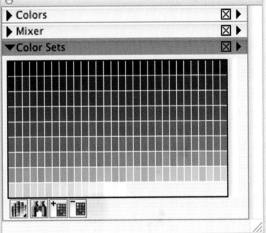

Figure 4.3

Classical colors.

Sample a medium gray-green from the Color Sets Palette. (See, it was useful sooner than you thought!) Choose Canvas > Set Paper Color. Create a Quick Clone—can you guess what the background color will be?

Tool Marks

Let's use Oil Pastel for this painting. It will produce a smooth, creamy effect without bristles. Notice that Oil Pastel variants come in different tip shapes. I like the Chunky group with an elliptical tip, but you might prefer round, rectangular, or triangle-shaped tips. Size is more important than shape for the preliminary painting. At a 30-pixel size, using Clone Color, you can "rough in" the basic tree trunks and major branches with very few strokes. Figure 4.4 shows this stage, with Tracing Paper on.

Size and Detail

When you paint with Clone Color or Cloner variants, the bigger your brush the less detail you will have. In general, you'll want to begin with a large brush size for the broad strokes. Details can be created later with smaller size variants.

Figure 4.4
Roughing it.

Continue painting the upper section of the image with a 30-pixel Oil Pastel, using directional strokes that follow the main branches. Most of the dark upper section of the trees will have no detail at all, just some color variation. Use shorter strokes in a variety of directions to fill that area. Figure 4.5 shows how fresh and lively this can look. Don't try to make your work look exactly like mine, and don't even undo strokes you don't like. Paint right over them—just as in real life!

The same basic technique works well on the grass and that strip of trees in the background. You are deliberately eliminating details, but not variety. Don't make your brush strokes too smooth. Figure 4.6 is developing nicely.

Figure 4.5
Fresh paint.

Figure 4.6
Rough enough.

Artistic License

That bright horizontal strip I like so much is practically pure white, and I think it will look too harsh if I clone it in. Let's turn off Clone Color and choose a lemony yellow from the Color Sets Palette. Paint those negative shapes in the same quick-and-dirty style we've been using. At this point I created a soft edge for the painting to blend with the paper color. That is done automatically with another cool feature on the Underpainting Palette. It's the Jagged Vignette on the Edge Effects menu. Turn the default 25% down to about 10% to make the edge this narrow. Figure 4.7 shows the sunny yellow strip and the vignette edge.

Let's soften some of the edges inside the painting, too. Switch to a Blender for that purpose. I used the Soft Blender Stump 20 to gently smooth and smear over the harsh color transitions.

You're ready to bring in some details now: bright patches of sky and grass. Using a smaller Oil Pastel, about 20 pixels, dab on some spots of color, using Tracing Paper for reference if needed. We expect sky to be blue, but there isn't any sky blue in the color set. There's no law against going outside the color set, but I found some pinkish tones that worked out fine. Figure 4.8 has these bright spots added. All they need now is a bit of softening with the Blender. The finished painting appears at the beginning of this lesson.

Figure 4.7
Soften the edges.

Figure 4.8
A few bright spots.

You fill Up My Screen

Working with a large image? Make the most of your screen space with Screen Mode Toggle (Cmd/Ctrl+M). Toggle visibility of all palettes with the Tab key. Make zooming and scrolling easy with keyboard controls. The spacebar gives you the grabber hand, while spacebar +Cmd/Ctrl lets you click to zoom in. Add the Option/Alt key to that combination to zoom out. It's important to look at your image at 100 percent magnification fairly often, as some textures and effects look weird otherwise. Double-click the Magnifier tool to get 100 percent size instantly.

Spring Flowers

Who knew when I went out for fresh bagels this morning that I would find the inspiration for a fresh project? You'll find the photos of daffodils and California poppies (shown in Figure 4.9) in the Nature > Flowers folder on the CD that accompanies this book.

We'll use the photos for guidance, but there will be no tracing or cloning and no attempt at realism or exactness. Look ahead to Figure 4.14 to see the loose, sketchy style we are after. Layers will be very helpful for planning and developing this piece.

Figure 4.9
California blooms.

Layout Layers

Create a new blank white canvas with a vertical format. I'm working on a 2 x 3 inch canvas (dimensions always specify width before height) at 300 dpi, a good size and resolution for printing in this book. Of course the image will fill my screen and spill over a bit. You might want to use a lower resolution so you can see the entire image at 100 percent.

There is a custom palette called Watercolor Sketch available for this project in the Palettes and Libs (libraries) folder on the CD. Import it using Window > Custom Palette > Organizer. It has three variants: Flattened Pencil for preliminary sketching, Scratchboard Tool (a Pen variant) for line drawing, and Pointed Simple Water from the Digital Watercolor category to apply color.

Add a new layer to the canvas for a rough layout sketch. Notice that the stems and leaves of the daffodils are tall and strong compared to the fluffy bush under the California poppies. That suggests a layout with the poppies below the taller flowers. Don't forget the tiny daisies at the base of the daffodils. The scribbles in Figure 4.10 indicate all of those elements.

To change your color set, click on the Library Access button at the bottom left of the palette. Use the Open Color Set command and switch to Vivid Spring Colors. It's found in a long list of color sets in the Painter Support Files folder, and it's perfect for this project. Add another layer and use Digital Watercolor to dab in rich yellow, orange, and a couple of shades of green. Be sure to use the Gel or Multiply composite method for your color layer so the pencil marks can show through. I added a second color layer so I could overlay more color to suggest shading. Figure 4.11 shows my Layers Palette at this stage.

Figure 4.10
Springtime for scribblers.

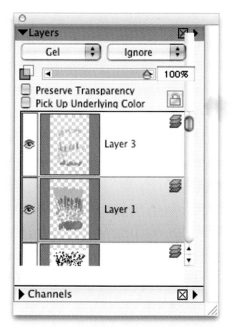

Figure 4.11
There's always room for Gel mode.

Layer Management

Rename your layers with the Layer Attributes dialog. It's available in the Layers Palette menu or by double-clicking the target layer. You can group layers by Shift-clicking to select them, then using the Group command. To commit a group to a single layer, use the Collapse command. Easy access to Layer commands is available with the left-most icon at the bottom of the Layers Palette.

On a new canvas, practice sketching some of the flared shapes of the poppies and the more complex structure of the daffodil flowers. Depending on your viewing angle, the poppies either look like bowls or overlapping triangles. Notice that the daffodils have a six-pointed star base and a central hollow tube with a frilly edge and a stamen or pistil (or whatever) sticking out (I know it's a sex organ of some kind).

If you feel a need to start by tracing, make a Quick Clone of the Daffodils_2 photo and do a few quick blossoms with the Flattened Pencil. Then draw some from memory with Tracing Paper turned off. Simplify the structures as you work and use different viewing angles. Avoid any tendency you might have to achieve perfection! Figure 4.12 shows some practice flowers, both traced and freehand.

Figure 4.12
Cover your stamens or pistils, please!

Drawing the Line

Make a new layer for the line drawing. Turn off the visibility of your color layer(s) and reduce opacity of the layout layer to about 30%, just enough to serve as a guide for the sections of your artwork. Choose the Scratchboard Tool and make some practice strokes with it to get the feel of working with different amounts of pressure. You might want to make the tip smaller, so adjust its size either with the slider in the Property Bar or with the left bracket key ([). Don't forget to use Preferences > Brush Tracking to customize the sensitivity of your Wacom tablet, as needed.

Sketch several flowers, daffodils above and poppies below. Keep it loose and lively. A cartoony style is fine. Some vertical strokes will establish the long stems and leaves of the daffodils. A few bushy scribbles will work nicely at the base of the poppy section. Figure 4.13 shows this work in progress, with the layout layer opacity at 30%.

Quick Eraser

Imperfections are charming for this kind of work, but if you must remove some bits, turn the Scratchboard Tool into an eraser by simply holding down your Option/Alt key while clicking on the background white. Sample black again to return to drawing more flowers. This is so much quicker than actually switching to an Eraser variant.

Figure 4.13
Loose and layered.

Just Add Watercolor

When you finish the line drawing, you can eliminate the preliminary layers. A quick way is to hide the visibility of unwanted layers and use the Drop All command in the Layer menu. Now add a new layer for fresh color. Remember to choose Gel or Multiply for the composite method. The Digital Watercolor variant provided in the custom palette for this project is Pointed Simple Water. It is an ideal choice for applying blobs or streaks of color in as casual and imperfect a style as your line work. See Figure 4.14 for my effort. I added a second color layer so I could build up some tonality here and there. It turns out that the trick of making the Scratchboard Tool into an eraser works for this Watercolor variant as well. So, I was able to wipe out areas of color where they weren't needed.

Figure 4.14
Spring has sprung.

Variations

You'll need to drop the layers into the canvas to save your finished work in JPEG, TIFF, or other file formats. But keep the layered version in RIFF so you can explore some options, now or later. For example, try turning the opacity of the line layer way down for a more delicate effect. Or hide the line work altogether for a soft, nearly abstract color study. Consider creating a completely new line drawing using the color layer as inspiration. Figure 4.15 shows my color work with the line layer at 20% and hidden completely.

Pay Attention to Paper

The image with only color showing makes paper texture obvious. I happened to have the custom paper I made for an earlier project as the current texture. I didn't notice it as I was working, and it's too late to change now, unless I want to completely repaint the color layer. It looks okay, but if I had been paying attention, I would have chosen a more pleasing paper, such as French Watercolor. Many variants reveal paper texture even if they don't have "grainy" in their name.

Figure 4.15
Primavera variable.

Bayside Scene

Figure 4.16 shows a pastel drawing with some ink line accents that I created last year in Painter IX. The photo source, called Tiburon_Pier.jpg, was taken in an upscale little town north of San Francisco and shows the city skyline in the distance. You'll find it in the Places folder on the CD. Let's recreate the drawing together. I expect this variation to be a bit different because I'm using a newer version of the software, and because I'm older and wiser. Also, according to some even older and wiser philosopher, "You can't step into the same river twice." I'm sure that applies to San Francisco Bay.

Figure 4.16
Dock of the bay.

Prepare!

There are several things we ought to do before we start to render this scene. That wide expanse of sky is not very interesting, so let's minimize it. Use the Crop tool and your judgment about how much of the image should be eliminated. I decided to include a bit more of the water and pier structure on the right side this time.

I also want to work with more exciting colors for my new variation. You can enrich the muted tones of the photo by simply increasing saturation. In Painter X, use the Photo Enhance section of the Underpainting Palette and choose Intense Color. Notice that the Saturation slider has moved completely to the right for maximum effect. Users of earlier versions of Painter can accomplish exactly the same thing with Effects > Tonal Control > Adjust Colors. Drag the Saturation slider all the way to the right. Figure 4.17 shows the colorful result, as well as my suggestion for cropping.

Figure 4.17
Cropped and saturated.

Make a Quick Clone of the prepared photo. Unlike with last year's version, I will be using Clone Color, taking color and value information from the source image, so we won't need a color set. There is a custom palette for this project in the Palettes and Libs (libraries) folder on the CD, called Pastels and Chalk. (Import it with the Custom Palette Organizer.) It includes three sizes of drawing tools, a grainy blender, and two paper textures (Rough Charcoal Paper and Pebble Board). Figure 4.18 shows this custom palette. The drawing tools are arranged from left to right in decreasing size. The Square Chalk variant is about 14 pixels.

Square Hard Pastel 25   Square Chalk   Pastel Pencil 3   Grainy Blender 10

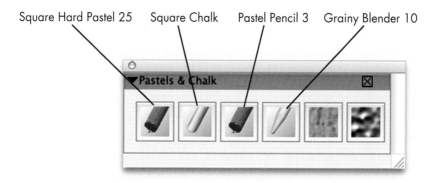

Figure 4.18
Pastels palette.

Custom Icons

The brush icon in a custom palette is the icon for the category. I chose a Chalk variant rather than another Pastel for the middle size, partly to avoid having three identical icons in a row. I'm pretty sure you can create new icons to avoid this kind of situation, but I didn't want to bother.

Simplify!

Although we'll be using dry media and achieve a very different look, the basic approach used in the trees painting at the beginning of this lesson still applies. That is, you'll begin by reducing the image to simple shapes and add some detail at the end.

The larger the brush (or stick), the less detail that is possible. Choose Square Hard Pastel 25 and Rough Charcoal Paper from the custom palette, or just find them on your own. Turn tracing paper opacity to about 70% so you can see your work more easily. With Clone Color enabled in the Colors Palette, make some of the (mostly) horizontal and vertical shapes in the image. Leave plenty of white space, remembering that less is more, as in Figure 4.19.

Figure 4.19

Less is more, more or less.

Clarify!

At this stage, it's pretty hard to tell what the subject of this drawing is, but a few more strokes will make things clearer. Continue adding (mostly) horizontal and vertical dabs, but use a smaller size this time. The Square Chalk, at about 14 pixels, is ideal for the next level of development. But wait just a moment. Suppose you add your medium detail on a new layer. Even better, how about having the first stage of the drawing on its own layer so it can be reduced in opacity while you work (letting you see the source photo more easily)?

Turning the canvas image into a layer is not a problem. Choose Select > All (Cmd/Ctrl+A), Edit > Cut (Cmd/Ctrl+X), followed by Edit > Paste in Place. This will make the canvas blank and create a new layer with the canvas contents in the correct position. Now make a new layer for the next stage. Reduce opacity of the "original" layer to about 50% and stroke in some windows, pier pilings, and other elements of similar size with the medium-sized chalk. Don't forget to enable Clone Color.

Toggle tracing paper often so you can see your work. You might need to decrease opacity of the tracing paper for faint items like the pale blue city skyline. Ignore thin lines and tiny details—you've probably guessed we'll put those on a separate layer. Switch to the Pebble Board paper when you add strokes for the water. Figure 4.20 shows the medium details added.

Figure 4.20

Getting clearer.

It's time to add another layer for fine detail. Use the Pastel Pencil 3 to pick out a few thin lines here and there, such as flag poles and railings. Don't use Clone Color for this layer, but do switch between black and white. Some details require removal of color. Actually, you're not erasing, but painting opaque white over existing color or over other layers. Figure 4.21 has a close-up of a section with some fine detail added. I really like the patterns made by roof tiles.

I included a Blender variant in the Pastels and Chalk custom palette in anticipation of a need to soften some of the edges in the original layer. You've been saving each stage of the project (haven't you?), so you have nothing to lose by experimenting with a bit of blending.

Grainy Blender 10 is a good choice for this kind of softening. You can get some very subtle effects, even when pressing fairly hard. The rough texture is an important feature of this piece, and too much smoothing could spoil the effect.

Figure 4.21

Details, details!

Decisions, Decisions!

Now comes the really hard part—deciding when you're done! Add a little sky with your large Pastel variant, using a couple of shades of blue sampled from the artwork. Soften up some of those edges, too. Figure 4.22 has my finished artwork. But is it really finished?

Figure 4.22
Close enough!

Keep your layered versions for a while at least, making it easy to change things. Changes include more than adding or taking away painted strokes. For example, try switching the composite method of the medium detail layer to Gel or Multiply. All the marks made on that layer will appear darker because they are combined with the colors on the layer below. Did you reduce opacity of the first layer when you created the medium details? You might want to adjust that opacity for the final version, also, to lighten up the entire image.

What's Next?

Well, that's enough fresh air for one day. Let's go back indoors.

If you have worked these lessons in order, you have tackled increasingly complex subjects, and you are probably developing more confidence with Painter tools and features. At least you're willing to take more risks. Actually, we've only scratched the surface of Painter's capabilities. (Don't go looking for a Surface Scratching variant, although I'm sure you could make one with just the right combination of Brush Controls!)

You may already have some favorite Painter tools and a preference for certain subjects to draw and paint. Are you also developing a style of your own? I encourage you to be open to working in a variety of styles, choosing among them when you begin a new project. Painter makes it so easy to switch from pencil sketching to oil painting to chalk drawing. Don't be surprised if I ask you to combine all of those techniques, and more, in one project.

5 Drawing People

$f$ruit, furniture, flowers, and now (drum roll, please!)—faces! Seems like a much higher level of difficulty, doesn't it? If your hand slips when you're drawing an apple or a wing chair, not a problem. But a tiny little mistake when you're working on a portrait, and suddenly, he's not your Uncle Ira anymore! Also, when you're sketching a still life, your subject is unlikely to criticize your work, especially if you plan to use your model as a snack later. Incidentally, the French term for still life is *nature morte*. Just thought I'd mention that.

Setting aside the fact that accuracy and proportion are critical for successfully drawing the human face and figure, we still have the same basic elements to work with: lines, shapes, tonality (light and shadow), and texture. There are familiar approaches as well, whatever our subject: choose a composition, simplify the forms, and then develop enough details to engage the viewer.

Portrait

Begin with a close-up photo of someone you don't know so that you're not influenced by your feelings for (or against) the person. It's a good idea to avoid young children (their faces aren't developed yet) and exceptionally good-looking people (for so many reasons, including damage to your self-esteem). Find the photo you want to work with, or join me in using this candid (unposed) headshot of JohnG. The original, available in the People > Heads folder on the CD, is on the upper left of Figure 5.1. The directional lighting makes it a good choice for drawing and painting, and I like the soft focus. I made a sharpened version, too, with Effects > Focus > Sharpen. In the Sharpen dialog, choose the Gaussian aperture and set the amount around 11. Sharpening reveals more texture and color variation in the skin. That could prove interesting later on.

Figure 5.1
Bring me the head of JohnG!

Changing Resolution

Did I warn you not to increase the resolution of an image without decreasing its size proportionally? That's because you usually won't be improving quality. Well, here's an exception to that. If you have a small and/or low-resolution image to use as a clone source for a drawing or painting, increase the resolution as much as you like *before* you create the clone copy. Your brush strokes (whether using Clone Color or not) will be at the higher resolution.

Two Heads Are Better Than One

We will create a couple of portraits of John in different styles. I prepared two preliminary versions from the Underpainting Palette. They are shown in the bottom row of Figure 5.1. The Sketchbook Color Scheme is on the left. The other version has two Underpainting effects applied simultaneously: Modern Color Scheme and Desaturate from the Photo Enhance list. These prepared images are also provided in the People > Heads folder.

Be Prepared

Let's begin with a sketch using just two colors, dark brown for shadows and white for highlights, with tinted paper for mid-tones. If this sounds familiar, you used a similar approach for a tonal study of the pear in Lesson 2. Here are the basic steps for setting up this type of sketch:

- Pick a neutral gray from the color picker or sample a medium tone from the source photo.

- Use Canvas > Set Paper Color.

- Make a Quick Clone of the source image (yes, the blank background will be the new paper color).

- Choose your paper texture, brush variants, and color set.

- Practice a few strokes on a blank canvas and, if needed, adjust tablet sensitivity with Brush Tracking.

I'll use Charcoal Paper for this drawing, but you might like something smoother or rougher. There is a custom palette available in the Palettes and Libs folder on the CD, though you probably don't need that much hand-holding anymore. It's called Tonal Sketch and has Square Chalk (14 pixels), Sharp Charcoal Pencil 5, and Pastel Pencil 3. Except for a few broader strokes in the background, I ended up using only the Pastel Pencil 3 for the entire sketch. I like the firm, grainy quality of this variant.

Stages in my head study are shown in Figure 5.2. Using a dark color, establish the major lines and shadow shapes. Work with strokes that vary in direction, following the planes and curves of the face. Begin to add a few highlights with white strokes, using the same sketchy technique. Develop the likeness by toggling tracing paper on and off frequently and changing the opacity of tracing paper as needed. Create visual interest by leaving out some lines or details. I like the expression of John's mouth in this photo, so I make that area the focus of more detail. Avoid a solid outline around the head, which can make the drawing look flat. My finished drawing looked a little anemic, so I punched it up using Effects > Tonal Controls > Brightness/ Contrast. An increase in contrast along with a decrease in brightness worked nicely.

Figure 5.2
Three stages of John.

With only two colors, it's easy to switch between them using the Eyedropper access trick (Option/Alt key) while you're sketching. Even better, make a color set with those two colors, plus the paper color. Open the Color Sets Palette and use the command at the top of the popup menu: New Empty Color Set. Figure 5.3 shows the menu commands and icons needed. With your dark color current, click on the Add Color icon at the bottom of the palette. Switch to white and click Add Color again. Sample the paper color and add it to your new color set. Make the swatches much bigger with the Swatch Size options at the bottom of the menu. I chose 48 x 48 pixels.

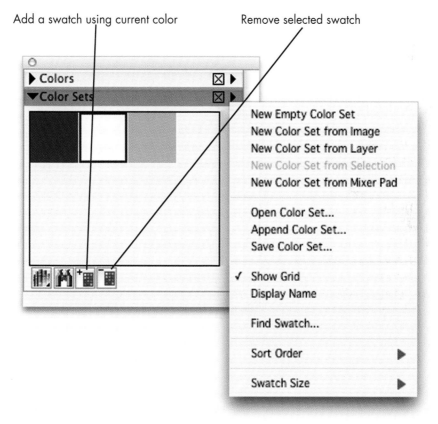

Figure 5.3
Color Sets popup menu options.

Why include paper color in your color set? To cheat! That is, you can make corrections by drawing over unwanted dark or white lines with the paper color. This works only for variants that function using the Cover method, as opposed to the Buildup method. Chalk, charcoal, and pastels all use the Cover method as part of their basic behavior. To find out what method your current variant uses, or to change it, open the General Controls by selecting Window > Brush Controls > Show General, as shown in Figure 5.4. As long as you're up, take a peek at some of the other settings, such as Dab Type and Stroke Type. These will make more sense when you get to Lesson 8.

The Shadows Know!

The version of John with Modern Color Scheme and Desaturation throws much of his face into deep shadow. To exploit that, let's use a painterly style reminiscent of Rembrandt, whose self-portrait at age 22 is shown in Figure 5.5. *Chiaroscuro* refers to the way this old master brought forms out of the shadows. Or maybe it's a fancy Italian dessert.

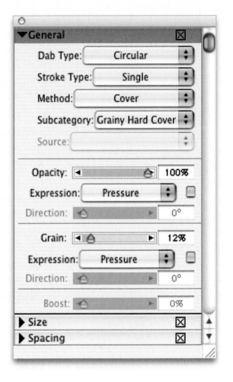

Figure 5.4

Cover me!

Figure 5.5

Discover me.

Definition

According to Wikipedia.org, *chiaroscuro* (Italian for *clear-dark*) is defined as "a bold contrast between light and dark." *Tiramisu* (Italian for *pick-me-up*) is made from ladyfinger cookies, espresso coffee, mascarpone cheese, eggs, cream, sugar, marsala wine, cocoa, and rum.

Open JohnG_ModernDesat.jpg. Do you recall applying a few thick Impasto strokes on the loveseat image in Lesson 3? This time we'll use nothing but Impasto all over the image. Find the Smeary Varnish variant in the Impasto category. Or you can import the custom palette for this project, called Impasto Smear. There are three items in this palette. Two are Impasto brushes, and the third is a Cloner variant that has a pleasing Impasto quality, the Oil Brush Cloner.

Use File > Clone to make a copy of the image. Don't use Quick Clone because you don't want the copy deleted. You'll be working directly on the copy, blending edges and mixing adjacent colors while applying thick juicy brush strokes.

Depth Charge

Painter's Impasto depth effect looks strange at magnifications other than 100 percent, so plan either to work on this image at actual size or to view it frequently at full size. Consider changing size or resolution of the source image before you make the clone copy.

Notice that the Resat (resaturation) value for Smeary Varnish is zero, indicating that no new color will be applied. Play a bit with this brush to get the feel of it and consider tweaking its behavior. Figure 5.6 shows a practice area made using the Paint Bucket and a gradient fill. The long squiggles show that this brush picks up color at the beginning of a stroke and continues to smear that same color for the entire length of the stroke. You can take advantage of that fact when you work. Notice in the upper left how color strips are blended with short overlapping strokes. The three straight horizontal strokes at the bottom show different values for the Feature setting in the Property Bar. The default value is 3.0, used in the center stroke. Higher amounts create more space between bristles, and reduced amounts compress bristles. The magenta swirl at the top of the image shows what happened when Resat was turned up, allowing the current selection in the Colors Palette to be applied.

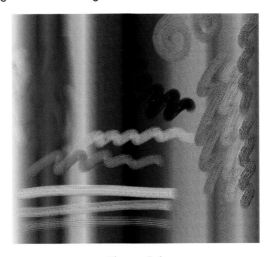

Figure 5.6
Smear me once, shame on you!

Another variable that influences the look of an Impasto stroke is the amount of depth. This control is not available on the Property Bar but is found in the Brush Controls Palette via the Window menu. Figure 5.7 shows the Impasto Control Palette. Notice that the default depth for Smeary Varnish is 12%. The vertical squiggles on the extreme right of the practice area show the result of increased values for depth.

Begin working on the clone copy with Smeary Varnish. I applied a variety of strokes to the background and John's shirt, shown in Figure 5.8.

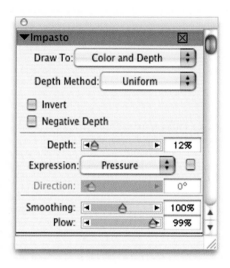

Figure 5.7

In-depth analysis.

Figure 5.8

Smear me twice...

Safety Net

Since you are not tracing or using Clone Color when you smear, are you wondering why you needed to clone the image in the first place? It's so that you can bring back any lost details in a painterly style. That's what the Opaque Round Impasto brush in the palette is for. It has 99% Resat. So just enable Clone Color, and you're good to go (back). Try the Oil Brush Cloner for a slightly different kind of "back stroke."

So with the Clone Color safety net in place, you can feel free to smear to your heart's content! In general, short strokes will work better, especially on details in the face. A smaller brush size will enable more control for those details. Use the bracket keys for quick size changes. As with other techniques, it's a good idea to pay attention to the curves and shapes of your subject and use them to guide your brushwork. Also, soften harsh edges. Figure 5.9 has my finished painting. Rembrandt's reputation is safe.

Figure 5.9
Have some chiaroscuro with your espresso.

Self-Portrait

Artists have drawn and painted themselves since the invention of the mirror. You've probably seen numerous self-portraits by Van Gogh. Even when he couldn't afford to hire a model, his own face was always handy. Portraits don't necessarily have to be restricted to the head and shoulders. Torsos and even the entire body can be included, but the head will usually be the most important element.

You're invited to set up a mirror next to your workstation, or if it's more comfortable, work from a recent photo of yourself. I'll be working with the image in Figure 5.10, part of a series of photos taken by Joseph Schaller while I was creating live digital caricatures at a wine gallery in San Francisco. Several photos from this series are included in the People folder, and you have my permission (and Joseph's) to work with them.

Figure 5.10
The artist at work.

Be Yourself

Feel free to work with more than one reference photo, combining the best aspects of them in your digital portrait. Plan to use a painting style compatible with your personality and artistic instincts. If you tend to prefer a loose, casual style (as I do), don't hold back. If your work is generally tight and controlled, stick with that approach—but you might also want to consider that life is short.

You have at least a nodding acquaintance with several techniques by now. I invite you to use any combination that appeals to you and to experiment freely. That's what I intend to do. Before you begin, try some new color schemes or enhancements for your photos in the Underpainting Palette. When you begin painting, use the RIFF format so you can make iterative saves easily. Start with File > Clone (not Quick Clone) so you'll have a safety net.

Work in layers for maximum flexibility. I want to have the clone copy of the photo on its own layer. To do that, choose Select > All, followed by Edit > Cut, then Edit > Paste In Place. This will automatically create a new layer with the photo in the same position. Now I can turn the opacity of the photo down while I work on other layers.

On a new layer, I'll make a line drawing with Dry Ink. If you've been practicing the pressure control exercises I recommended in Lesson 1, you know where to find this variant. If not, I won't punish you by making you look all over for it—it's in the Calligraphy category.

Dry Ink creates a luscious, bristly line whose width is very responsive to pressure. If I were stranded on a desert island and could only have one Painter brush variant, it would be Dry Ink. My line drawing layer is shown in Figure 5.11, and the Layers Palette at this stage can be seen in Figure 5.12. Notice that I have locked the photo layer to prevent drawing on it accidentally. To lock or unlock the current layer, click on the padlock icon on the Layers Palette.

> ### I'm Glad You Asked
>
> Why not just use Tracing Paper to see the original photo at reduced opacity? Because when Tracing Paper is, say, 50 percent visible, your painting is 50 percent visible. The only way to see your working image accurately is to turn Tracing Paper off completely. Not a problem when the photo is on its own layer.

Figure 5.11

What's my line?

Don't Throw Away the Key

When you want to save your image in a variety of file formats that don't support layers, you'll have to use the Drop All command to flatten the image. This won't work if any of the layers are locked.

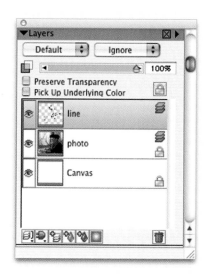

Figure 5.12

Layered look.

Color is next, and that requires another layer, using Gel or Multiply mode so the black lines will show through. The line drawing has a cartoon or comic book style (check out the "speed whiskers" around the Wacom pen), which suggests adding flat color to the skin area. I'll do that with Dry Ink. Other areas on the color layer will be left blank for now. The photo layer is no longer needed, and I'll delete it to reduce file size.

Mix and Match

I really like the colors in the scarf, and I can make them into a color set by dragging a lasso selection loosely around that area (nobody wants a tight scarf) and then using the Color Sets menu option to make a New Color Set from Selection. I added a couple of useful colors that are not present in the scarf (white and bright red) by choosing each of them in the color wheel and clicking the Add Color icon at the bottom of the Color Sets Palette. Figure 5.13 shows this color set, as well as a great Painter feature we haven't worked with yet, the Color Mixer. Incidentally, if the color set looks a bit different, it's because I turned off the grid of white lines that normally separate the color swatches. Just toggle the Show Grid command in the Color Sets menu.

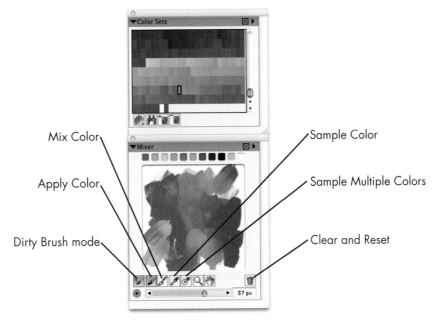

Figure 5.13
Welcome to the Color Mixer Palette.

The Color Mixer is available as part of the Colors Palette in the Window menu. It functions much like a traditional mixing area on an artist's palette: blobs of paint are placed next to each other, and a brush or palette knife is used to mix them partially or blend them completely. Then the brush is loaded with a color or a combination of colors that can be applied to the canvas. Most of the tools at the bottom of the Color Mixer will be familiar to you, but a couple of them need to be explained. The Brush icon can apply the current color and also mix colors already on the mixer pad. If Dirty Brush mode is enabled, the mixing brush will begin with the current color and blend it with the colors on the pad. The Eyedropper tool, as expected, samples a color from the mixer pad and makes it the current color for painting. Now here's the interesting part: the eyedropper with the circle at its tip can sample more than one color. For maximum effect, click it on a part of the pad where two or more colors meet. So why is this exciting? There are a couple of Brush categories that can paint with more than one color at a time. I'm talking about Artists' Oils and (new in Painter X) RealBristle Brushes.

Take a few minutes to play around with the Color Mixer and some of the Artists' Oils and RealBristle Brush variants. Did I mention you can save not only the colors created on the mixer, but also the entire mixer pad? Load the mixer pad I'll be using for this project from the Palettes and Libs folder on the CD. It's called PurpleRedOrange. While you're at it, help yourself to the custom palette I made for this project, called Ink-Oil-Real, shown in Figure 5.14. It includes, from left to right, the following variants (category names are also shown):

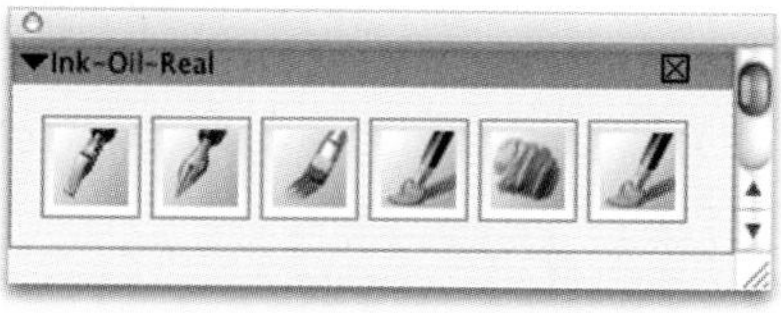

Figure 5.14

Clumpy and smeary and (like) real.

- Calligraphy > Dry Ink

- Pens > Scratchboard Tool (smooth pen and ink for details)

- Artists' Oils > Clumpy Brush

- RealBristle Brushes > Real Oils Short

- Impasto > Smeary Varnish (back by popular demand from the JohnG painting)

- RealBristle Brushes > Real Flat (all RealBristle Brush variant names start with "Real"—I don't think this name means it's *very* flat)

Figure 5.15 has some test strokes made with the Artists' Oil and RealBristle variants from my custom palette. The two vertical strokes in red and mauve were made with the Clumpy Brush. I like the random variation in spacing of the bristles. That's what "clumpiness" means in Painter's terminology. Notice that the position of colors in a stroke depends on the direction used to apply it. Also notice in curved strokes that the width of the brush is unchanged. The RealBristle Brush variants, on the other hand, are capable of a variety of stroke shapes, based not only on the shape of the brush but also on response to the tilt and bearing of your Wacom pen. The purple and brown strokes were made with Real Oils Short. The orange and yellow strokes were done with Real Flat.

Testing Brushes

Before you begin working with a brush category or variant that's unfamiliar to you, create a new document for testing it under a variety of situations: paint over different backgrounds using different colors, pressure, and direction. Make some long strokes to see if pigment fades out. Drag a stroke over changing colors to observe the smeariness of the brush. See what happens when you change the value of controls in the Property Bar, then use Restore Default Variant in the Brush Selector Bar menu.

Figure 5.15
This is only a test.

I made the test canvas in Figure 5.16 to explore the behavior of RealBristle Brush strokes when dragged across different colored backgrounds in different directions. Both of the variants I'm using pick up color at the beginning of the stroke and carry it along. The effect is stronger with Real Oils Short, due to its much higher values for Bleed and Blend. I'm quite liking the look of this test canvas and thinking it could come in handy when we create some abstract paintings in a later lesson.

Figure 5.16
Bleeding and blending.

Let Yourself Go

Multicolor Clumpy Brush strokes look great on the scarf and not bad on the hat. Figure 5.17 has a detail of this state. I'm going to use my artistic license (before it expires) and explore some painterly effects on the background. What follows is a combination of experimentation (what some people call "trial and error" I like to call "trial and success") and a bit of inspiration. I saved half a dozen layered stages as I created this piece, using Iterative Save. They are all available in the Lessons folder on the CD for your examination.

I retrieved some background color from the abstract paintings behind me in the photo, using Dry Ink with Clone Color enabled. I liked some of these strokes: the area behind my hat and back, and the brown squiggles near my arm echoing the line of my right sleeve. Figure 5.18 shows that more work was done on the face, with darker skin tone and a couple of highlights added. Also added was a pinkish hue on the nose and ears. Another tool was dragged into my custom palette, a Blender variant for smoothing these skin tones and the rough strokes on the hat. Colorful reflections on the eyeglasses were made with the Scratchboard Tool.

Figure 5.17
Getting colorful.

Figure 5.18
I love that hat!

The face is finished, but I will take the pink color off the ear. I also take out the yellow and orange stuff I had cloned in from the abstract painting in the photo. Those just aren't my colors. Then I have an inspiration. There is a perfectly good abstract painting with my favorite colors waiting for me in a practice file I just made for testing new brushes (similar to the one in Figure 5.16). So I create a new layer for it and paste it in. Figure 5.19 shows the changes. The shading on the hands was drawn with some scribbly hatching by the Scratchboard Tool.

Figure 5.19
Practice makes perfect (almost).

91

Experimenting once again, I use Effects > Orientation > Distort to manipulate the shape of the abstract painting layer so it will fit the space better. Then comes my second inspiration—I unlock the line layer and draw a stylized monitor with Dry Ink. After a little erasing, everything kinda fits together. Figure 5.20 could be the final stage, but I confess to doing a bit more fiddling. The image at the beginning of this lesson shows a later version with a few more changes. For example, I realized I hadn't used Smeary Varnish at all, so I worked on the abstract painting layer with it, mostly to blend color over the black background.

Figure 5.20
We're done (maybe).

People in a Scene

I'm guessing you've worked hard in this lesson and could use a bit of time relaxing on the beach. How about a compromise. Let's draw and paint other people relaxing on the beach. If you know how to keep sand and saltwater out of your laptop, then go out on location. If not, pick out a photo or two from my Waikiki collection in the Places > Honolulu folder on the CD. There are several good choices to consider. I'm torn between beach_couple.jpg and beach_lady.jpg. Figure 5.21 shows my dilemma. I really like the figure of the elderly lady, but it's a bit stark with no background other than sand. The sky, trees, and the strip of people sunbathing under beach umbrellas in the other photo would make a good setting for her. What to do?

Figure 5.21
On the beach.

Image Manipulation

Painter provides most of the same tools for editing photos that you'll find in Photoshop or Photoshop Elements, though some are named and organized a bit differently. We can easily make a composite using the Lasso tool (it's a roommate of the Rectangular and Oval Selection tools) followed by the Copy and Paste commands. Figure 5.22 shows how nicely (and quickly) these two photos can be blended. The layered RIFF file is also available in the Honolulu folder, as beach_lady_layered.

Well, there is one thing about the composite that's not quite right. The post that begins just at the feet of the couple now appears to end 20 yards or so out toward the ocean in the beach lady image. You can simply ignore it because the photo is only going to be used for reference. But if it really bothers you, or you want to practice some retouching techniques, here's how to eliminate it.

Choose the Rubber Stamp tool, which shares a space in the Toolbox with the Cloner. You'll use this to apply pixels from one area of the image to another. We'll clone clear sky, shaggy roof, and sand over the post. Holding down the Option/Alt key, click on the point you want to designate as the source. A number 1 will appear alongside a green dot. Now begin paint-ing over the target area that you

Figure 5.22
The best of both beaches.

want to cover. Figure 5.23 shows the process. The section on the left has the source indicated, and some of the sky and the shaggy roof has been painted out. Establish a new source pixel for sand to clone over the bottom of the post.

Figure 5.23

Now you see it, now you don't.

Where Are the Clones?
They're Already Here!

Painter IX and earlier versions don't have a Rubber Stamp tool, so use a Cloners variant. Choose Straight or Soft Cloner and establish the source pixel as above by clicking with the Option/Alt key held down.

The best way to fill in the missing part of the umbrella is to simply paint with the Scratchboard Tool and reds sampled from the umbrella. That result, in the middle section of the figure, should be enough for our purposes. But if you must cover that last bit of post, here's how I did it. I cloned in a sunbather from another position and cloned in the striped towel from the extreme left to cover the "missing" face of the woman lying on the sand.

Saltwatercolor

We'll choose brushes from the Digital Watercolor category, and then plunge in a bit deeper than we did with the Spring Flowers project in the previous lesson. Applying the Watercolor Color Scheme from the Underpainting Palette produces the effect in Figure 5.24. This file is provided in the Lesson 5 folder on the CD as beach_lady_compWC (*comp* stands for composite). Make a new color set from this image.

Figure 5.24
Ready to paint, finally!

Use Window > Custom Palette > Organizer to import the Watercolor Sketch custom palette for this project. Click on the paper swatch in the custom palette to establish French Watercolor Paper for your texture, or choose a different texture from the Paper Selector. Make a Quick Clone of the prepared photo so you can use tracing paper as a guide. On a new layer, make a rough sketch of the major lines and shapes in the scene using the Flattened Pencil with a dark brown from the color set.

Choose Pointed Simple Water from the custom palette. But first, make a "scratch" canvas to experiment with some of the Property Bar settings for this brush. Increase the Wet Fringe value to get the effect of pigment pooling at the edges of a stroke, a distinctive feature of traditional watercolor. Move the Diffusion slider a few points to the right and get a completely different effect: the edges of the stroke feather into the background, revealing paper texture. Figure 5.25 has a stroke made with the default settings, followed by increased Wet Fringe, then a stroke with higher diffusion. Notice that increasing diffusion eliminates the Wet Fringe look. Use any brush settings you prefer for the next step, roughly laying down the color areas on another new layer. See this stage combined with the pencil line layer in Figure 5.26.

Figure 5.25

Is my fringe wet?

My watercolor strokes don't extend to the edges of the canvas, making an irregular vignette edge that is more pleasing than a geometric rectangular shape. Sunbathers in the distance are just scribbles, and that's enough for now. You won't need tracing paper any more, but keep the photo source open as a reference.

Figure 5.26

Simple rough color.

Let's develop richer shadows, color variation, and a few details with some of the other Digital Watercolor brushes. The following suggested variants should help you navigate through the long list of possibilities in that category:

- Wash Brush

- Fine Tip Water

- Gentle Wet Eraser

- Coarse Dry Brush

- Salt

Is It Worth the Trouble?

Painter's Digital Watercolor takes some experimentation to find the right combination of variants and technique to fool the eye. Close observation of traditional watercolor paintings will help you create the digital equivalent. Notice, for example, areas of exposed white paper and the vibrant "accidents" of overlapping transparent colors.

The Wash Brush is fine for painting broad areas of color and works nicely as a transparent wash over other colors, even on the same layer. If you want to remove watercolor pixels, you'll need to use a "wet" eraser rather than a variant from the Erasers category. I applied some Gentle Wet Eraser strokes near the bottom left of the color layer for more pleasing edges. To create the fringed shadow, I switched to Fine Tip Water, which functions as an eraser when white is the current color. The Salt variant creates a good imitation of real-life effects. When you sprinkle coarse salt granules on wet watercolor, they soak up the pigment, leaving a distinctive pattern behind. Notice the effect of Salt on sand in a detail of the current state in Figure 5.27.

Figure 5.27

Sand, salt, and fringe.

Fine Tip Water works well for adding details. You may want to add another layer for details or richer color overlays. I used Coarse Dry Brush to paint contour strokes on the trees and for texture on the shaggy roof. When your watercolor layers are well developed, consider erasing some of the lines in the original pencil sketch. My finished painting is shown in Figure 5.28. Notice how I handled the far off sunbathers, with little dabs of color. Examine the layered version in the Lesson 5 folder on the CD.

Figure 5.28
Pass the suntan oil.

What's Next?

Congratulations on completing the basic lessons in digital painting! In the lessons to follow, you'll find advanced projects and a more intimate look at brush controls. You'll also be invited to play with some exciting Painter features that go way beyond simply imitating natural media.

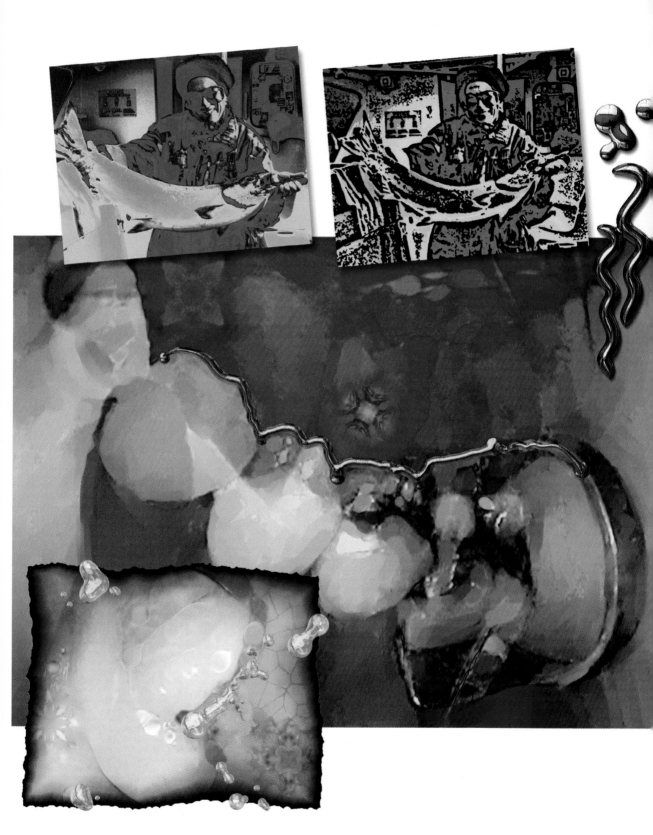

Beyond
the Basics

Figure 6.4
Come up and see my woodcuts.

Faux Silkscreen

A silkscreen print, or *serigraph*, is created by squeezing ink through a fine mesh onto paper or t-shirts, fabric, whatever. An image is created because parts of the mesh screen are protected from the ink with some kind of resistant fluid, or *resist*. As with relief prints, several passes can be made using different screen designs and different colors. Photographic images can be transformed into silkscreen graphics, and these are most successful when the original images are simplified.

Well, Painter has a Serigraphy effect in the Surface Control group, right near the Woodcut effect. But we're not gonna use it. We can get better control and more exciting options using another combination of effects to imitate a silkscreen print. Let's start with one of the snakeskin shoe photos in the Things > Shoes folder on the CD.

Figure 6.5
Open-toed elegance.

Make a copy of the shoe on another layer, as you did for the Woodcut exercise. We'll use Effects > Surface Control > Apply Screen on the new layer. (It doesn't matter if you start with the canvas image.) The Apply Screen dialog, shown in Figure 6.6, allows you to reduce the full range of tonality to just three flat colors—any three colors you want. You also get to determine the threshold for both color changes. Click on a swatch to pick a color, then experiment with both Threshold sliders. Choose settings that will enhance the snakeskin texture. Be sure to switch to Image Luminance in the Using field. My results, shown in Figure 6.7, include some accidental-looking bits of pink in the background. These are great, and don't even think about eliminating them! They give a realistic, gritty quality to the image.

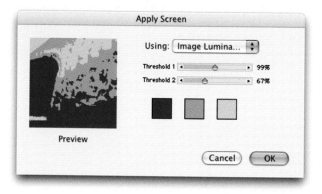

Figure 6.6
I hope they come in my size!

Figure 6.7
Pretty in pink.

This is already a bold graphic that could be used in a print ad or poster. But you still have another layer to play with. Choose Effects > Tonal Control > Posterize for the second copy, with four levels. Now comes the fun of exploring different composite methods. You might like several combinations, so be sure to save each one. Can you guess which composite method is used in Figure 6.8?

Is It Art or Advertising?

Those categories overlap considerably, and it's not so much what the image looks like or how it was made, but how it's used. Since Andy Warhol exhibited large prints of Campbell's soup cans, bringing "pop" culture into the realm of contemporary art, all bets are off.

Figure 6.8
If the shoe fits...

Vector Values

Speaking of categories overlapping, there is some common ground between pixel-based programs, such as Painter or Photoshop, and vector-based products (Adobe Illustrator reigns supreme in that arena). If you're not sure how these approaches differ, see my brief explanation in the Appendix.

Although all Painter images are ultimately pixels, there are some tools you can use to take advantage of vector-like capabilities, such as dynamic (editable) Stroke and Fill. Figure 6.9 shows where these tools are located.

Paths to Enlightenment

Use either the Rectangular or Oval Shape tool to drag the corresponding shape on your canvas. With the Move tool engaged, resize or reposition a shape as often as you like. When you tire of ovals and rectangles and want something a little more exciting, use the Quick Curve tool to draw any irregular shape. All shapes are composed of a path (a sequence of curves or line segments) and anchor points that can be altered with the Shape Selection tool.

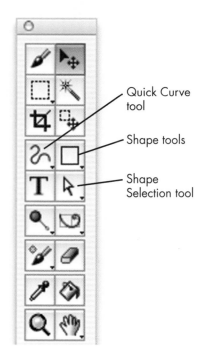

Quick Curve tool

Shape tools

Shape Selection tool

Figure 6.9
Vector selector.

The Pen Is Mightier

The Pen tool, not to be confused with the Pens category of brushes, shares a space in the Toolbox with the Quick Curve. This is the ultimate vector tool, capable of making any complex shape by clicking and dragging anchor points. It takes a good deal of practice to develop proficiency with this technique, so I recommend Quick Curve for the less-than-perfect approach in this book.

Each shape you make automatically creates its own separate layer with a distinctive icon that differs from an ordinary layer. Figure 6.10 has an oval and rectangular shape and a Quick Curve shape. I've added a bristle brush stroke on a standard layer so you can compare the layer icons as well as the contrast between vector flatness and pixel juiciness.

The Shape menu provides several commands for managing shapes. When any Shape tool is active, the Property Bar offers choices for Stroke and Fill. Those color swatches give you access to the current color set or the option to load a different color set. Check boxes let you determine whether Stroke and/or Fill is on or off.

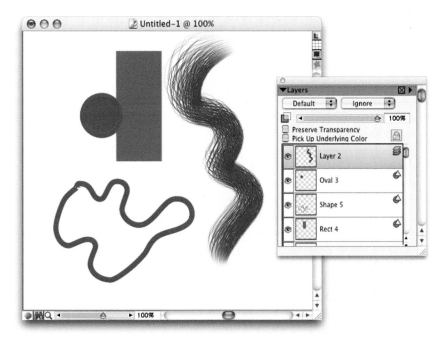

Figure 6.10
Shape up!

My irregular shape appears again in Figure 6.11, this time with a yellow stroke and a lavender fill. The Shape Selector tool is active, so you have access to the individual anchor points along the path. The target point is red, indicating it can be moved or its "wings" can be dragged around in order to alter the curves on either side of the point. Make some Quick Curve shapes and play around with strokes and fills, as well as manipulate anchor points and their wings. If you want to change the width of a stroke, you'll need to open the Set Shape Attributes dialog from the Shapes menu.

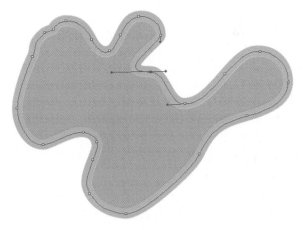

Figure 6.11
You are the wind beneath my anchor points.

111

Paths for Alignment

So you see how it's possible to prepare precise paths. Now what? With your Brush tool active, take a look at the three icons near the left edge of the Property Bar. The default mode is Freehand strokes, but you can also choose Straight Line strokes. The third option is Align to Path, and that's the key to combining vector precision with painterly style.

Make your own simple graphics using the vector tools in Painter or import existing Illustrator files. Use File > Acquire to open images that are in either .ai format (Adobe Illustrator) or .eps format (Encapsulated Postscript). Those .ai files will have to be in Illustrator 8 format in order to be recognized by Painter. When you use the Acquire command, Painter takes a moment or two to *rasterize* the image to make it compatible with the pixel-based environment. You'll see the paths in your Layers Palette as Shapes or Groups of Shapes. At this point you are free to change the size or resolution of the image.

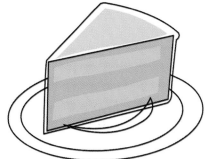

I've already rasterized a vector illustration for you to work on, shown in Figure 6.12. It's cakeslice.rif, in the Things > Food > Just Desserts folder on the CD. Some of the shapes have fills, and all of the shapes have thin black strokes to help you see your work in progress.

This is an excellent opportunity to use the Liquid Ink category, which functions on its own special layer. I chose the Smooth Bristle variant, which isn't really smooth. If I had the time, I'd rename it "Not So Smooth Bristle."

Figure 6.12
Fill in the filling.

What's in a Name?

You can change the names of brush variants and even reorganize them into different categories if you wish. Just navigate to the Corel Painter folder on your hard drive, then choose Brushes > Painter Brushes. Then find the variant you want to rename. Each brush has three component files: .nib, .stk (stroke), and .xml. All three must be renamed or there will be trouble. Incidentally, those tiny (4k) JPEG files associated with category names are the icons for the categories. Yes, you can replace them with your own icons. Make a Rectangular selection of the image you want for a new icon and use the Capture Brush Category command in the Brush Selector Bar popup menu.

With the Align to Path option engaged, draw around each of the shapes using any colors you like. My working image appears in Figure 6.13. I temporarily turned off the fills by unchecking them in the Property Bar, with the Shape Selector tool active.

Those accidents of overlapping color are fine, enhancing the hand-painted look. Don't try to fix them if you get some. The finished cake has the fills turned on again and all the stroke lines turned off. At this point the image is ready to be flattened and saved to any format. Keep a RIFF file with shapes intact in case you want to redo it with different brush variants. All Figure 6.14 needs is a cup of coffee. You'll find one in the Vector Files folder on the CD.

Figure 6.13
Blue plate special.

Figure 6.14
Piece o' cake!

It's Only a Mask

In traditional printmaking or airbrush painting, areas can be protected from paint or ink with a mask. These can be made from tape, cardboard, or self-adhesive frisket paper cut to the precise shape needed. Earlier in this lesson, I mentioned the use of liquid resist for masking portions of a silkscreen mesh. It shouldn't surprise you that in digital art creating masks is much easier.

Pixel-based applications like Painter and Photoshop provide several tools for selecting portions of the canvas to accept painted strokes or effects. Whatever isn't selected is, by definition, masked. You can make selections based on geometric shapes or draw freehand selections around an irregular area using the Lasso tool. A sophisticated selection tool that has no counterpart in traditional media is the Magic Wand, which selects all pixels in a defined color range. Figure 6.15 shows where the Selection tools are located on the Toolbox. The Rectangular Selection tool is currently active. Its roommates are the Oval Selection tool and the Lasso. Notice the Selection Adjuster tool, which allows you to move or resize a selection marquee.

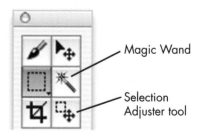

Magic Wand

Selection Adjuster tool

Figure 6.15
Selection, selection, selection.

The Select menu offers handy commands for altering and managing selections. There is also a special Library Palette, the Selection Portfolio, with a collection of common (and not-so-common) selections you can simply drag to the canvas. Open the Selection Portfolio by selecting Window > Show Selection Portfolio and load the Lettering selections from the Extras folder in the Painter X application folder. If you're using an earlier version, choose the heart or star selection from the default portfolio shown in Figure 6.16.

When the Ants Come Marching In

An active selection of whatever shape has a moving marquee like an animated dashed line. The cute nickname for this is *marching ants*. You might want to turn off the marching ants (without losing the selection) to see your work better. The Hide Marquee command in the Select menu has a keyboard shortcut: Shift+Cmd/Ctrl+H.

Once you have a selection, you can paint in it without the need to be careful at the edges—there's no way you'll go outside the lines. You can also fill a selection instantly with a solid color, a gradient, or a pattern, using either the Paint Bucket tool or the Fill command in the Effects menu. An especially useful command in the Select menu is Stroke Selection. This will automatically paint the edges of your selection with the current color, using the current brush variant. Yes, that sounds a bit like the Align to Path option.

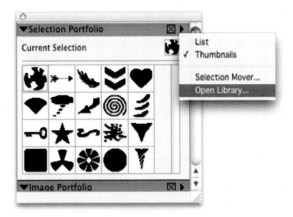

Figure 6.16
Just drag and drop.

Fancy Schmancy

Figure 6.17 has a sampler of creative ways to work with a selection. Here are the techniques used, top row from left to right, then bottom row.

- Gradient fill.

- Fill with current color (pink), then Stroke Selection with Impasto > Acid Etch brush.

- Select > Invert (this makes the selection a mask so it is protected) then paint freely around the letterform with an Artists' Oil variant.

Figure 6.17
Say "Aaaaa."

- Fill with the current Pattern (Silver Tubing Pen). Then copy and paste to make the item a new layer. Apply Effects > Objects > Create Drop Shadow.

- Choose Lotus Petals as the current pattern, then Stroke Selection with Pattern Pen Masked (the Pattern Pen category will be discussed shortly).

- Fill with solid red. For the 3D bevel use Effects > Surface Control > Apply Surface Texture, using Image Luminance.

There hasn't been much drawing and painting in this lesson, and your mouse would have worked fine for most tasks. Now it's time to pick up your Wacom pen again to explore the amazing Pattern Pen category. Take a look at the strokes in Figure 6.18. With only two exceptions, all these strokes were made with the Pattern Pen Masked variant. The difference between the masked and the "not masked" variant is demonstrated with the two Double Helix strokes. The blue background that is part of the Double Helix pattern is masked out when you use Pattern Pen Masked. In the lower right of the figure, Wave Mosaic is also painted both masked and—the other way. ("Unmasked" can't be the right word for a stroke that includes a strip of background color. It makes me think of somebody being forced to reveal his or her true identity.) The potential for decorative, expressive, and whimsical uses of Pattern Pens will be explored in the next lesson.

Figure 6.18
Strokes of genius.

Can't find the Snakeskin or the Blonde Braid?

I gathered my favorite patterns from several versions of Painter into one collection, or library. It's called Rhoda Patterns and is available in the Palettes and Libs folder on the CD that came with this book. Just use the Open Library command in the Pattern popup menu. You can easily reshuffle patterns from several libraries by using the Pattern Mover utility. Same kind of function is provided for papers, gradients, and so on.

Airless Airbrush

The ideal brush category for working with selection masks is Airbrushes. Traditional airbrushes spray tiny droplets of pigment mixed with compressed air. The instrument connected to that compressed air source is a metal device with a nozzle and a small reservoir for pigment. It has a couple of tiny wheels for finger control of the size of the spray and the density and coarseness of the droplets. It takes quite a bit of practice to get skilled with a traditional airbrush. Painter lets you shave months, even years, off that process. Make a new canvas for trying out several of the Airbrush variants.

Figure 6.19 shows some airbrush practice. Check out the realistic response to the tilt and bearing of your Wacom pen as you change its angle and direction. The two purple strokes, made with the Pepper Spray variant, were done with the pen held at a steep angle to the tablet, in opposite directions. The green strokes show what happens when an airbrush is moved rapidly but lingers a bit at the beginning and the end of a stroke: pigment keeps on spraying. The blue star was made with the Fine Wheel Airbrush. I sprayed a bit at the lower left of the selection, then used Select > Invert so I could spray outside of the star. I switched to the Soft Airbrush 40 to make the very smooth pink strokes and the heart. Both the heart and the yellow propeller show a basic technique for creating the illusion of depth: spray a slightly darker color for the shadow side, slightly lighter for the highlights. Remember to be consistent with your imaginary light source.

Figure 6.19
Fresh air.

The imaginary landscape in Figure 6.20 was created with a combination of smooth and coarse Airbrush variants and a few selection masks made with the Lasso tool. A couple of the masks, "mountains" and "bushes," were saved for repeated use. RIFF files showing the development of this piece are available in the Lesson 6 folder on the CD, and they include the saved selections. When you use the Save Selection command, a new channel is created. Open the Channels Palette, where you'll find icons for saving, loading, and inverting them. Those options are also available in the Select menu.

These are the Airbrush variants I used for different parts of the artwork.

- **Soft Airbrush 50**—Mountains, dark green hills, foreground flowers, cloud.

- **Pepper Spray**—Light green grass, snow on mountain tops, sky.

- **Tiny Spattery Airbrush**—Yellow flowers on the green grass.

- **Coarse Spray**—Foreground pink and fuchsia bushes.

Figure 6.20
Purple mountain majesty.

Recreate this whimsical landscape with me. Start with a white canvas 3 x 4 inches at 300 ppi. Open the RIFF file of the final stage, AirbrushLandscape_005 in the Lesson 6 folder so you can use it as a guide. Feel free to borrow the selection masks I saved or make similar ones with the Lasso tool—they're quick and easy. Figure 6.21 shows the Channels Palette for the completed piece, and Figure 6.22 has my "mountains" mask (the marching ants are resting temporarily).

Figure 6.21

Channels tuned in.

Figure 6.22

Ants march over mountains.

Move your Lasso selection into position with the Selection Adjuster tool. Spray a light purplish-blue color for the furthest mountain range, then switch to the Selection Adjuster to move the selection lower for the next group of mountains. Use a slightly darker color for this section. Save the selection in case you need it later. For a little variety, before spraying the third set of mountains, I flipped the selection horizontally. There doesn't seem to be a way to do this automatically, so with the Selection Adjuster tool active I dragged one edge across to the opposite side, then pulled the second edge out the other way. Kids, don't try this at home...and don't confuse this transformation with the Invert command, which deselects all selected areas and vice versa.

I made a new Lasso selection for the green hills. Some lighter green highlights were added with a large-sized brush, stroking from above the selection for more control. Figure 6.23 shows this technique.

Figure 6.23

The hills are alive.

Figure 6.24 shows a lot of progress, with sky added and some snow sprinkled on the mountains, aided by loading the mountain selection once again. (I knew it would come in handy.) The foreground bushes were sprayed in using a new selection, saved as "bushes."

Now let's add a fluffy cloud, sprayed white and then given a gentle shadow and sunny glow at its top. As a finishing touch, the foreground could use a bit of detail. I scribbled a Lasso selection to suggest a flower shape, gave it the shadow-and-highlight treatment, and then inverted the selection so I could spray a darker pink behind it. A couple of these Lasso scribbles were worth repeating, so I dragged them to a new position with the Selection Adjuster and repeated the process. It was easy to make a few new flower scribbles, too. I like the irregular edges of this painting, giving the viewer a glimpse at the process. So it turns out that airbrush art doesn't have to be slick, smooth, and realistic. And it doesn't necessarily have to feature either sports cars or what used to be called "pinup" girls.

Figure 6.24
Sky and bushes added.

What's Next?

The advanced features we played with in this lesson are worthy of
a lot more investigation, and you are cordially invited to explore
them more fully with or without my directions. In lessons yet to
come, you'll have an opportunity to combine and hone your skills
while you delve into even more exciting and exotic brushes, features,
and effects.

7 Mixed-Up Media

I mentioned "mixed media" way back in Lesson 2. It refers to artwork that combines two or more techniques that are traditionally separate. Even putting pencil strokes on a painting qualifies. Imagine the excitement early in the 20th century when *avant garde* artists were pasting photos, newspaper clippings, and small objects on their canvasses! Painter takes the mixing of media to a whole 'nuther level.

Isn't That Special!

You had a taste of painting with patterns in Lesson 6. There are several other brush categories and variants that allow you to go past mixing media and into the realm of special effects. Figure 7.1 shows a sampling of strokes you'll want to try, and there is a custom palette in the Palettes and Libs folder on the CD to give you some encouragement. It's called Special Effects and is shown in Figure 7.2.

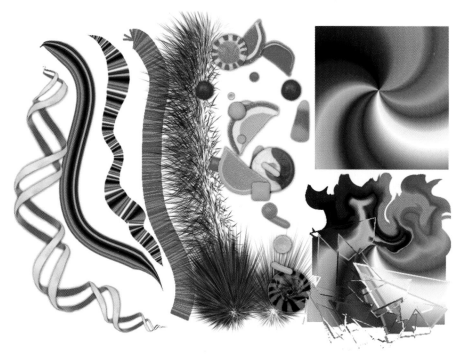

Figure 7.1
Wild, weird stuff.

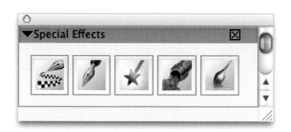

Figure 7.2
Special Effects starter kit.

If that stroke on the far left in Figure 7.1 looks familiar, then you haven't forgotten Pattern Pen Masked. The pattern used here is called Double Helix, but I think of it as Twisted Linguini. Moving to the right, you'll see a stroke made with a Pens variant, but this one doesn't use the current color—it paints with the current gradient! This particular gradient is called Vivid Colored Stripes, and it was used with the Paint Bucket to fill two rectangles at the far right, in order to demonstrate some distortion effects, Hurricane (in the Distortion category) and Shattered (an F-X variant). Gradient pens come in two flavors, and both are shown in Figure 7.1. Grad Pen uses all the colors in a gradient and squeezes them down the stroke like toothpaste. Grad Repeat Pen performs as advertised, repeating all the colors in strips that run perpendicular to the stroke. I don't think they can do that with toothpaste—yet.

Anatomy of a Brush

The next stroke has the charming name Piano Keys, and it resides in the F-X category. I like using this brush to demonstrate how to change the behavior of a variant using Brush Controls. Choose Piano Keys from the Brush Selector Bar or the Special Effects custom palette and start a new canvas big enough to let you do a lot of test scribbles. With a bright color at medium saturation, make a couple of strokes so you'll have the default qualities of the brush visible to compare with changes. Open Brush Controls from the Window menu. We'll be looking at several sections of this long palette, and you won't be able to see all of them at once. That's okay; just expand or collapse them as needed with the little black triangle next to the name of the section. Let's begin with the top two controls, General and Size, shown in Figure 7.3.

General gives you the most basic info about any variant. The Dab Type for this brush is Captured, which means it is an irregular shape or group of pixels, such as a small drawing. The shape in this case is a very thin rectangle. You can get an individual Piano Keys dab on your canvas if you tap your Wacom pen tip on the tablet. The Size Controls also show the shape of the Dab, in the Brush Dab preview window. (If that window shows a circle, tap on it once, and it will show the captured shape.)

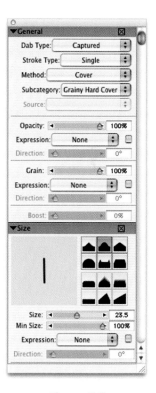

Figure 7.3
Top two Brush Controls.

Grab a Dab!

Several other members of the F-X category use captured dabs: Fairy Dust, Fire, Shattered and Squeegee. Yes, you can make a new and unique brush dab for your current variant. Create it, then select it with the Rectangular Selection tool. Use the Capture Dab command at the top of the popup menu in the Brush Selector Bar.

Skip to the Opacity setting and notice that it is at 100% and the Expression field shows None. This means there can be no variation in opacity within a stroke. Click on the Expression popup menu to see the choices available for altering opacity. (These are the same choices you get whenever you see the Expression option in any of the Brush Controls sections.) Choose Pressure, and make a test stroke. Now your brush can respond to pressure input from your Wacom pen. Figure 7.4 shows my stroke with default settings at the top left and the pressure-responsive strokes at the top right.

Figure 7.4

Piano practice.

Close or collapse General Controls and take another look at the Size Controls. You can choose to vary the width of the stroke, but there will be no effect unless you reduce Min (minimum) Size to less than 100%. When Min Size is around 40% and Random is chosen for Expression, you get the jagged result in the blue stroke. (I'm just switching color between changes because it's more fun.)

Let's return to the original settings before you make the next few changes. You don't have to remember what those settings were, just use the Restore Default Variant command in the Brush Selector Bar popup menu. Close or collapse the Size Controls and expand Spacing and Angle.

Spacing refers to the space between dabs. Raising that value to about 40% gives you the picket fence look shown in purple. There are two important things to notice in the Angle Controls section: Expression is a function of Direction, and Ang(le) Range is the maximum 360 degrees. This makes it possible to paint a circle and have all the dabs radiate from the center. What happens if you reduce the Ang Range or change the Expression choice to something different? The gold color I used for strokes with Ang Range at 180 degrees and Pressure used for Expression look a bit like twisted ribbons.

Restore the default variant again and open one more control section, Color Variability. It's near the bottom of the stack of palettes and shown in Figure 7.5. With the HSV settings shown, you can see why the color variation in the Piano Keys stroke has darker and lighter shades of very similar colors. Value or Luminosity variation is relatively high at 15%, with Hue variation only 4% and no Saturation variation at all. Play with those sliders and see what happens. I chose the red color used for the original default stroke and raised Hue variation to 25% for the multicolored stroke at the bottom left. The last stroke has Saturation variability set to the maximum. As expected, the dabs range from rich vibrant red to neutral gray.

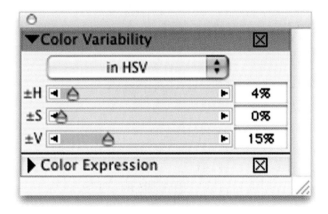

Figure 7.5

Color keys.

Spraying Color—or Candy

Go back to Figure 7.1 and let's pick up where we left off. That fluffy purple spray is the Furry Brush, also in the F-X category. Look at the General Controls for this variant to see that the Dab Type is Line Airbrush. The stroke does look like a spray of lines, and it behaves like members of the Airbrush category in a couple of ways. The spray is directional, depending on the tilt and bearing of your Wacom pen. The bottom of my Furry stroke shows that directionality. Also, the brush keeps spraying even when you're not moving it. That feature is called Continuous Time Deposition, and you can see it enabled in the Spacing Controls.

There is variation in the brightness of color in this spray of lines. A glance at the Color Variability Controls will confirm this, showing the V (value) slider is set to 25%. Figure 7.6 has another Furry Brush stroke with a couple of tilted bits that look like hedgehogs or porcupines. You can make dramatic changes in any variant by choosing a different Dab Type. I chose Circular Dab for the blue strokes. The value variation shows up clearly here. These circles are not all lined up perfectly along the stroke. That quality is called Jitter, and its control magically appeared in the Property Bar when I changed the Dab Type. With Jitter reduced to the minimum, you get the second blue stroke—circles all stacked up like poker chips.

Figure 7.6
A little dab'll do it.

How do you paint with candy corn, mints, and other tasty treats? The amazing Image Hose can spray not only junk food but images of any kind. The content is determined by your choice in the Nozzle Selector, available at the bottom-right corner of the Toolbox. As with all libraries (paper, gradients, patterns, and so on), you can load a different collection and reshuffle the items between libraries with the Mover utility. Now take a look at the variant list for the Image Hose category. Here's where you can decide whether you want image bits scattered around or marching in a line and whether to use pressure (P) direction (D), randomness (R), or other expression variables to control the size or angle of the images.

Load the custom library, Rhoda Nozzles, and practice using some of these techniques. My Image Hose sampler, shown in Figure 7.7, uses these nozzles and variants:

- Seashells: Spray-Size-P

- Koi: Spray-Size-P Angle D

- Nuts and bolts: Linear-Size-P Angle-D

- Candy: Linear-Size-R

- Sushi: Linear-Size-P

Those sushi slices on the left are too close together. How would you increase the spacing to display the center of each piece better? As for the single slice on the far right—that was done by tapping the tablet once, using a variant that did not specify size changes so that any amount of pressure would produce a full-sized sushi.

Figure 7.7
Nail that sushi!

Digital Caricature

Is there a practical use for painting with patterns, gradients, and pieces of food? Figure 7.8 should help answer that question. These are caricatures I created live with Painter IX at the 2005 convention of NCN (National Caricaturists Network). Celestia's big masses of curly blonde hair were quickly scribbled in with the linguini pattern (sorry, that's Double Helix). I used Double Helix again to make eye "sockets," which were then filled with a gradient. Karena wore a faux animal skin hat, so I painted several strokes of the Boa pattern to simulate it. And yes, each earring was done with a tap of the Sushi nozzle loaded in the Image Hose. So for someone doing business as Rhoda Draws A Crowd and creating live digital caricature entertainment at events, it's very practical.

Figure 7.8
Your eyes are like aquatic neon!

Even if you have no intention of becoming a professional caricature artist, you'll get better acquainted with Painter and develop critical observation skills by exploring this art form. Figure 7.9 has recent samples of my five-minute caricatures. Examine the image files for these in the Caricature Gallery of the Lesson 7 folder on the CD. There you'll find more examples, some as layered RIFF files, some with photos of the victims (sorry, I meant *subjects*) for comparison. Practice making caricatures with faces in the People > Heads folder. Most of these folks are already funny looking, so you'll have a leg up (or should I say "a nose up").

Figure 7.9
Five-minute faces.

Exaggerate and Simplify

A successful caricature expresses the essence of a person's face. Find at least one feature that is distinctive and "push" it. If the nose is long, make it longer. If the chin is weak, reduce it further. If the eyes are close together, move them in even tighter. Organization of the features in relation to each other is important, too. As with most other art projects, simplification is advised—leave out unnecessary details.

My digital caricature style has evolved over several years. After experimenting with many of Painter's flamboyant brushes and effects, I have simplified my technique. (The need to produce a finished drawing every five minutes, as entertainment for large groups, is a powerful motivation to simplify!) I prepare a template with two layers, and I begin by laying down the basic line elements with Dry Ink, that wonderful edgy variant from the Calligraphy category that you've been using for your warm-up exercises.

(If you haven't, it's not too late to start.) The second layer is for color, using Gel or Multiply mode for transparency. Dry Ink also works for splashing in the hair color or a facial tone quickly. Shading or additional color (rosy cheeks, eye shadow, and so on) is done with a Chunky Oil Pastel and a Blender variant. I chose Basic Paper for a smooth texture and Small Dots for beard stubble. Streaks in hair and glamorous eyelashes are created with a customized Scratchboard Rake.

Rake's Progress

The Scratchboard Rake, a variant in the Pens category, makes several parallel strokes. I added Color Variability using 10% variation for each setting: Hue, Saturation, and Value. There is a controls section for Rake variants, where you can change other behaviors. I saved my customized Scratchboard Rake as a new variant with the Save Variant command in the Brush Selector Bar popup menu.

A custom palette for my caricature style is available on the CD in the Palettes and Libs folder. It's called Rhoda Caricature and is shown in Figure 7.10. I don't use all the tools and commands on every drawing, but most situations are covered. Notice the inclusion of specific papers, gradients, and my favorite pattern. Three of the brush variants are from the Pens group, so they have identical icons, but I know which is which by their positions in the palette. Recall that items can be rearranged with the Shift key engaged. Commands are added to a custom palette with the Add Command option in the Custom Palette menu.

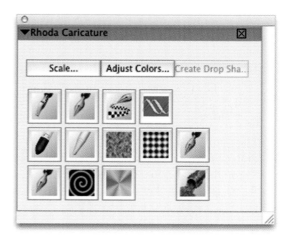

Figure 7.10

It comes with linguini on the side.

Look at Figure 7.9 again, and pay special attention to the woman with dreadlocks. Save time and amaze your friends when you use Pens > Barbed Wire 7 to make this type of hairdo in a few seconds. Let's examine this variant along with its cousin, Nervous Pen. Make a few test strokes and scribbles with each of them. Figure 7.11 shows three Barbed Wire 7 strokes on the left followed by two Nervous Pen strokes. The upper circular scribble was made with the Nervous Pen. The lower scribble was done with Barbed Wire in black and Nervous Pen strokes added using white.

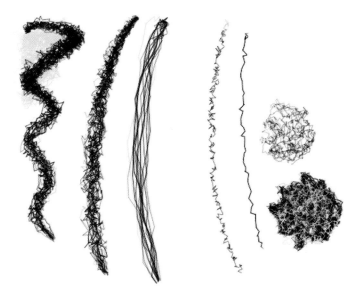

Figure 7.11
Bundles of nerves.

Barbed Wire appears to be a bundle of Nervous Pen strokes. The number of strands in these variants is determined with the Feature slider, available in the Property Bar. A higher Feature value results in fewer strands. The tangled, jangled quality of these brushes is a function of Jitter, which you saw earlier in this lesson. This time you won't see the Jitter control in the Property Bar, but you will find it in the Random section of the Brush Controls palette.

Jangled Nerves

Did your strokes have some variation in complexity or "tangledness"? The amount of Jitter responds to the speed of your stroke, with slower strokes producing dense tangles, while faster strokes stretch and smooth out the tangles. Are you guessing that the Expression variable for Jitter is Velocity? Then you'll be as surprised as I was when I saw None in the Expression field. Caffeine would have made more sense than that, but it's not an option.

The Eyes Have It

Eyes offer excellent opportunities for creative treatment, as shown in Figure 7.12.

Figure 7.12
Eye chart.

The two samples at the top of Figure 7.12 were painted with no special effects, if you don't count the Scratchboard Rake eyelashes. The middle row shows some of the fun that can be had with eyeglasses. If there are no leaks, the Paint Bucket can be used for gradient fills, and it's not necessary to give both lenses the same treatment. The big yellow lenses on the right also have Scratchboard Rake strokes around a "beady" eye to suggest a wild or confused expression.

In the bottom row, you'll recognize the sushi eyes from an Image Hose nozzle. The sand dollars and tomato slices were made in a very different way with a Painter feature I haven't mentioned until now. Open the Image Portfolio from the Window menu. Like the Selection Portfolio we used in Lesson 6, it is a library of items that can be dragged onto the canvas, but these items are images that create their own layers. The default collection is shown in Figure 7.13. You can easily make a new item for the Image Portfolio by dragging any selection from your canvas over to it, where you'll be prompted to give the new image a name. As usual for all Library collections, the Mover utility in the popup menu lets you create new libraries and swap items between them. Use the Open Library command to load the custom Portfolio Rhoda Favorites from the Palettes and Libs folder for the next project.

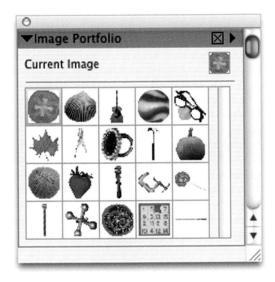

Figure 7.13
Your tomato slice is ready.

Figure 7.14 shows a photo of Nick, a good-looking young fellow even without the spike under his lower lip, and the first stage of my caricature. This photo is available in the People > Heads folder on the CD, so open it now and follow along. You can imitate my style if you wish or (even better) use your own approach. But I invite you to practice using some of the Image Portfolio items as you work.

Figure 7.14

Nick line.

By the time we get to Figure 7.15, I've added pink lips and bluish five o'clock shadow on the color layer. A marble has been dragged into place from the Image Portfolio, automatically creating its own layer. Now you can see why I include the Scale command on my custom palette. It saves time navigating through Effects > Orientation > Scale. This command allows you to type in the size percentage you want or drag a corner of the bounding box so you can (um) eyeball the amount of change.

You can use Create Drop Shadow to enhance the 3D look of the marble. The Layers Palette has created a group for Marble and Shadow, so the shadow occupies its own layer and can be manipulated independently. This feature (which is not available in Photoshop!) will come in handy very soon. For the second eye, all I have to do is switch to the Layer Adjuster tool (same as Photoshop's

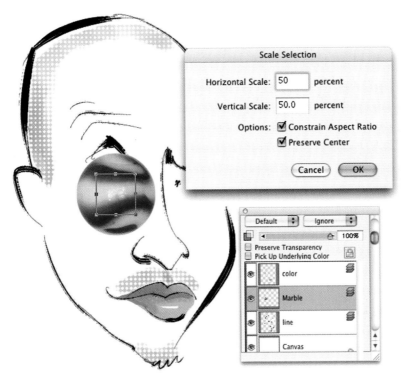

Figure 7.15
Marble eyes.

Move tool), hold down the Option/Alt key, and drag a copy of the Marble and Shadow group to its new location. A size reduction (85%) creates a forced perspective, moving the second eye back in space.

The Pencil in the custom Image Portfolio is an excellent shape for adding that lip spike, and it's especially appropriate because Nick is an artist. Use the Scale command to reduce its size to about 25% and change the angle of the Pencil with Effects > Orientation > Rotate. Now create a drop shadow. The top left section of Figure 7.16 has the Pencil in position, with just a little erasing done at the blunt end to simulate insertion (yechh!) into the flesh. The Layers Palette at this stage has the Pencil and Shadow group opened, with Shadow selected. Now you'll see how useful it is to have the shadow on its own layer. Use the Rotate command to change the drop shadow into a cast shadow for a much more convincing effect, also shown in the figure.

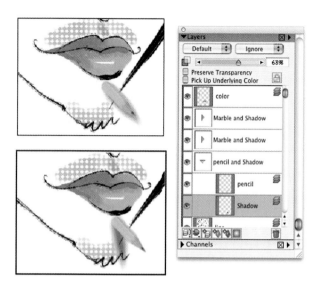

Figure 7.16
Shadow effects.

Plug In That Earring

The only thing missing now is Nick's earring. By now it shouldn't surprise you that Painter has a feature for creating realistic metallic brushstrokes, and here's the perfect opportunity to use it. We'll explore another unique set of special effects, the Dynamic Plugins. They reside in the Layers Palette and have an electric plug icon. Choose Liquid Metal from the Dynamic Plugins popup list (glance at some of the other choices for future reference). Figure 7.17 shows the Liquid Metal dialog box (which must remain open while you are creating Liquid Metal effects) and the new layer to accommodate those strokes. Practice making some strokes with the Brush icon selected, and switch to the circle icon to make metallic droplets. Notice the tendency for droplets to attract each other and run together! The Undo command won't work here, so if you want to remove a stroke or a droplet, use the arrow icon to select it and then hit the Delete/Backspace key. Strokes are actually made up of a sequence of droplets. You can see them individually by enabling Display Handles. Even after you click OK, a Plugin layer remains dynamic; that is, you can access the original controls by simply double-clicking the item in the Layers Palette. You can use Convert to Default Layer if you need to apply other brushes and effects. Figure 7.18 shows some test strokes and droplets.

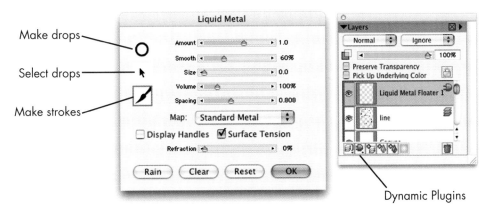

Make drops

Select drops

Make strokes

Dynamic Plugins

Figure 7.17
Dynamic duo.

Figure 7.18
Droplets and strokes.

The finished caricature in Figure 7.19 took longer than five minutes, I admit. That background was done with a Pastel variant and a texture not included on my custom palette, Square Hard Pastel with Pebble Board paper. How did I get the two-tone effect? Good question. I chose a dark pink sampled from the lips to roughly fill the area around the head, then I used the Invert Paper command in the Paper Palette popup menu. (*Invert* in this case means the light and dark areas are swapped). Yellow sampled from the pencil is the color used on the second pass.

Figure 7.19
Nick, your face is ready!

Painting with Chocolate

Liquid Metal, along with several other Dynamic Plugins, was introduced in Painter 5, and it is still amazing! With a little tweaking of the controls and preparing alternate source images for the reflection map, you can emulate a variety of liquids, including melted chocolate!

Consider the Source

Notice that Clone Source is listed along with the default Standard Metal map. In order to have a clone source that will imitate chocolate, I created an image called Chocolate_source.jpg, shown in Figure 7.20, along with the Gradient settings I used. This image is available in the Lesson 7 folder on the CD, but it's easy to make from scratch. Choose a dark chocolate for your main color and a milk chocolate for the additional color. Fill a blank canvas with the two-point gradient (select Windows > Library Palettes > Show Gradients) using the spiral style and one of the double configurations at the bottom of the Gradients Palette. Click inside your canvas with the Paint Bucket. For smoothing the spiral edges, use Effects > Focus > Soften.

Choose your chocolate gradient image in the File > Clone Source list. Make a new blank canvas in a horizontal (landscape) format and start a Liquid Metal layer. In the Liquid Metal dialog box, choose Clone Source in the Map list and paint with any combination of strokes and droplets. My effort is shown in Figure 7.21.

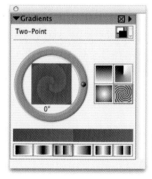 

Figure 7.20
Brown on brown.

Figure 7.21
How bittersweet it is!

Pattern as Clone Source

When there is no image designated as the clone source, Painter uses the current pattern as a default. When you realize that clone source and pattern can be interchangeable, it may occur to you that the Pattern Pen variants can paint with any open image designated as the source. When you choose Source in the Expression list for Brush Controls, variation in brush behavior will be based on the luminosity (brightness value) of the clone source or pattern.

I removed the chocolate droppings with the Metal Detector (I mean Selector). With the idea of a bar of chocolate in mind, I made a new standard layer and filled a rectangular selection with the double-brown gradient. I applied Effects > Objects > Drop Shadow to the Liquid Metal layer, accepting all the default settings, then I made adjustments to the new Shadow layer manually, reducing its opacity and moving it slightly. This stage is shown in Figure 7.22.

Figure 7.22
Satisfy your digital sweet tooth.

Fear of Commitment?

When you apply any effect to a Plugin layer, or when you attempt to paint on it with a brush variant, you'll have to commit it to a standard layer. If you commit, the electric plug icon for the layer is replaced by the default layer icon, and you can no longer make dynamic changes.

We'll add edge effects to the rectangle layer using other Dynamic Plugins. Burn, Tear, and Bevel World each require a target layer before they are available. Figure 7.23 shows the torn edge created with the Tear plugin settings in Figure 7.24. Adding a Bevel to the torn edges gives the illusion of thickness with crumbly edges in Figure 7.25. There are a great many settings in the Bevel World dialog box, and I'll leave you with the challenge of figuring them out on your own. This is the advanced section of the book, after all.

Figure 7.23
Chocolate paper.

Figure 7.25
Gettin' chunky.

Figure 7.24
Your settings may vary.

Blobs for the Masses

The dictionary defines *esoteric* as "things understood by or meant for a select few." The Esoterica collection in the Effects menu provides choices that aren't any more mysterious or arcane than items in the Surface Control menu. So don't let that label put you off—consider yourself a member of the inner circle. Just don't forget the secret handshake.

We'll use Esoterica > Blobs to create another chocolate-flavored effect. Artificially flavored, of course. Be sure the chocolate source image is still checked in the File > Clone Source list. Select a small rectangle around one chocolate swirl, something like the one in Figure 7.26, and use Edit > Copy (Cmd/Ctrl+C) to place it into the clipboard (also called the Paste Buffer, because this chocolate rectangle is now ready to be pasted).

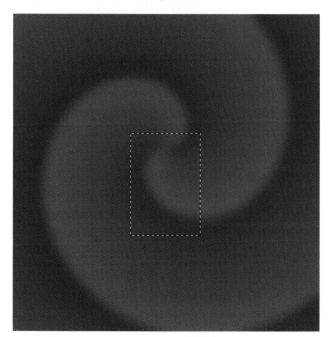

Figure 7.26
Ready to eat...er, paste!

Make a new canvas with a butterscotch or caramel colored paper, or fill a white canvas with that color. Choose Effects > Esoterica > Blobs. Figure 7.27 has the dialog box along with the caramel-colored background. Play around with numbers and sizes of blobs, and notice the choices for the Fill Blobs With field. The Paste Buffer contains that selection you just copied, and Pattern is going to be replaced by the entire chocolate image now serving as the clone source. If you choose Paste Buffer, your results should resemble Figure 7.28. There is randomness built into this effect, so your blobs won't match mine exactly, even with the same settings.

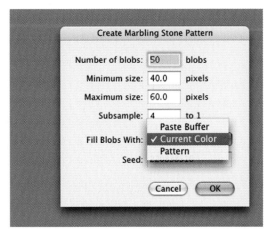

Figure 7.27
Prepare to blob.

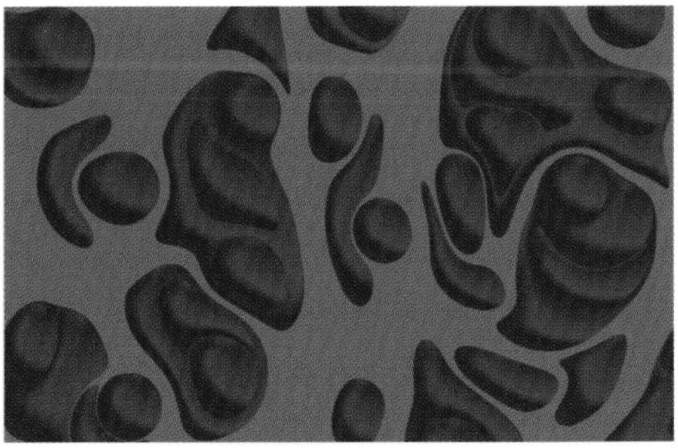

Figure 7.28
The lava lamp look.

Create Marbling Stone Pattern

If you're wondering why that's the title of the Blobs dialog box, it's because blobs provide the first step in creating marbling effects on paper or fabric. A traditional technique begins with dripping oil-based pigment onto a tray of water, where the natural resistance of the two liquids creates blob-like "stone patterns." The blobs can then be manipulated with straws or raked with combs to produce intricate designs. Painter provides such tools in the Apply Marbling feature, also available in the Esoterica group.

Okay, this is pretty esoteric after all, but why quit now? Go ahead and use the Apply Marbling feature (found in Effects > Esoterica > Apply Marbling) to your Blobs image. Rather than making all the settings by hand, use the Load button for some never-fail recipes. Figure 7.29 shows the Nonpareil Rake design at the top and the Horizontal Bouquet Comb below.

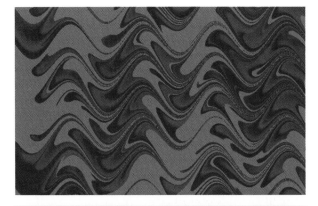

Figure 7.29
Fudge ripples.

What's Next?

After feasting on this smorgasbord, you may be overstuffed and need some time to digest everything—maybe even take a nap! Many of these special brushes are pretty spicy and might not be to your taste. Or you may find that some of the features are best used as a seasoning or a garnish, just a sprinkle to add zest to the dish. I could probably push this food metaphor for a few more courses, but I'll just suggest a little chilled sorbet to cleanse your ... palette!

There are still some amazing areas of Painter we haven't explored, and that journey isn't over yet. But for the next lesson, we'll get back to basics again: the basics of drawing and painting.

8 fine Art Challenges

Whether in action or repose, clothed or nude, classically rendered or abstract, drawings and paintings of the human body are the most popular subject matter for students as well as accomplished masters. In Lesson 5, you painted a scene that had some figures in it. In this section, you will strip away the palm trees and beach umbrellas and apply digital media to traditional life drawing techniques.

Figure Drawing

In a typical figure drawing class or workshop, an undraped model poses for increasing lengths of time, beginning with very short "gesture" poses lasting only a minute or two. Short poses are very energetic and active, exciting to capture quickly with a few strokes. For many years, I worked with charcoal sticks or oil pastels on big (18" x 24") sheets of paper. Nowadays, I'm usually the only one showing up with a laptop and Wacom tablet. My hands stay clean, and I don't have to worry about where to store all those drawings.

Find someone willing to pose for you, not necessarily naked. Or take your laptop and tablet to a figure drawing workshop. As a last resort, use photos from the People > Figure Study folder on the CD. Some of them have digital fig leafs where appropriate, so this book could qualify for a PG-13 rating. There is a series of Gypsy Roz in her belly dancing costume, giving you a range of poses with a similar theme.

Quick Study

Figure 8.1 shows a digital gesture sketch I did in about two minutes. This is one of about 160 poses I drew in 6 hours at a figure draw-ing marathon in 2006. There are many more examples from this session (and others) in the Lesson 8 folder on the CD. One of my favorite variants for fast figure drawing is Dry Ink, which is also my preferred brush for live caricature drawing (see Lesson 7). Not surprising, if you think of caricature as a facial gesture—a simplified and exaggerated impression of the forms and their relationship to each other.

There are exercises you can do to loosen up and other methods to develop accuracy. Let's see if we can combine a couple of them. A classic technique for practicing eye-hand coordination is *blind contour* drawing. The idea is to keep your pen or drawing tool on the paper or tablet and, *without looking at your work* (that's the blind part), slowly and deliberately make an outline of the subject. Whether it's a vase or a nude model, the process is the same, and improvement *will happen* if you practice.

Figure 8.1

Two-minute pose.

Naked Truth

Being forced to work this quickly encourages you to focus on the essence of the pose, skipping details. Just as important, this kind of practice helps you plunge into the process and ignore any self-doubt about your skill. After all, gesture drawings aren't meant to look good, and even if your effort sucks, there's another fresh opportunity to be successful every couple of minutes! "Process, not product" is the mantra you need to repeat to yourself if you are judging your work negatively or you feel "stuck."

I'll put a spin on blind contour drawing and recommend blind gesture drawing. Do *not* be slow and deliberate, and do *not* attempt to follow only the outer edge of the subject. So all we're keeping is the "blind" part. Figure 8.2 shows a couple of (mostly) blind gestures I made at a recent figure drawing marathon. I cheated a tiny bit, looking at my screen after making one blind contour line in order to place my Wacom pen in the right spot to do an additional line. Color was added later on a separate layer. After doing several of these, you'll be amazed at what you can accomplish with your eyes open!

Figure 8.2
Flying blind.

Do you have some favorite brush variants you tend to rely on over and over? I suggest you try a few brushes that are less familiar. Avoid the special effects brushes for now, and stick with natural media categories. I'll practice what I preach and stop using my old reliable Dry Ink for a while. A category I generally ignore, partly because I don't know how to pronounce it, is Sumi-e. These brushes imitate the effect of Chinese bamboo brushes. Figure 8.3 shows some test strokes with a few Sumi-e variants. I like the Tapered Sumi-e, which has a Static Bristle dab type and wide variation in size expressed with pressure.

A Method to My Madness

The Sumi-e category actually includes a couple of Dry Ink variants, and it makes sense to group them with other bamboo brushes. One important way these Dry Inks differ from the one in the Calligraphy category that I prefer is that their method is Buildup rather than Cover. Test what happens when you change between those two methods in the General section of Brush Controls.

Figure 8.3
Bamboo brushes.

Here's a checklist to help you prepare for a digital figure drawing session so you can work efficiently with minimal distractions.

- Make a custom palette with the brush variants and paper textures you want to use.

- Create at least one template canvas the size and color background you want, with a layer in Gel or Multiply mode to keep color separate from your line work.

- If you're working from photos, open at least 10 of them at once so you don't lose your concentration when doing fast gesture warm-ups.

- Use the Iterative Save function so you don't have to create new names for successive drawings.

Work for 20 minutes at a stretch, first with a series of 10 two-minute quickies, followed by four five-minute sketches, then two ten-minute drawings. Use any style(s) and brushes you like—just don't trace!

I'll use GypsyRoz14.jpg, shown in Figure 8.4, to demonstrate the development of a drawing through several stages. The first stage, a gesture in two layers (this time my eyes were open), is shown in Figure 8.5. Tapered Sumi-e was used for the lines, followed by some Dull Conte strokes on a transparent layer to indicate exposed flesh. We can use this as the basis for a more refined drawing, but I'll just consider it a preliminary warm-up.

Figure 8.4
Comanche name: "Dances with Scarves."

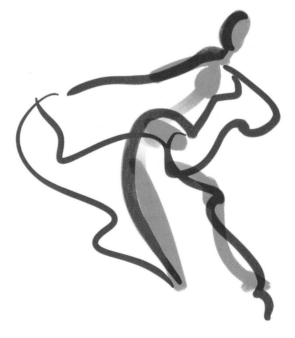

Figure 8.5
Gypsy gesture.

Proportional Response

Careful observation is important for life drawing, and knowledge of human anatomy is very helpful. Although the structure of bones and musculature is beyond the scope of this book, there are a few simple relationships for the relative length of body segments. Figure 8.6 shows Leonardo da Vinci's most popular and imitated image (not counting the *Mona Lisa*), the *Vitruvian Man*. It's based on a description of human proportion by Vitruvius, an ancient Roman architect.

I superimposed lines dividing the man's height into equal sections. Think of the height of the head as a unit for measuring relative distances on the body. This figure is 8 heads high. There is approximately one head distance from chin to nipples, and another head to the navel. The center of the body is at the groin. Knees are half-way between the groin and the soles of the feet. The "wingspan," or length of his outstretched arms, is equal to his height. These ideal proportions will serve nicely until you need to deviate from them for artistic purposes or your model has a different body type. Unless your model is standing up straight with all arms and legs in one plane, these proportions may have to be set aside in favor of actual observation.

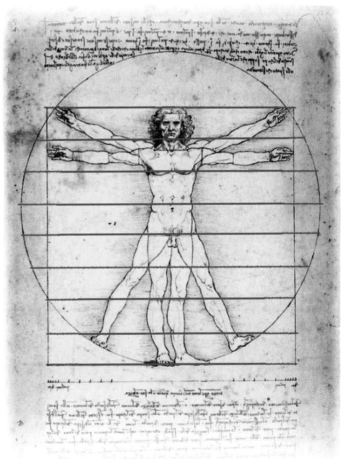

Figure 8.6
Vitruvian guy.

I was serious, earlier, when I told you not to trace for this project. Don't worry—there are things Painter can do to help with your observations. Grids and Guides, found in the Canvas menu, are useful for making measurements and judging angles. The source photo in Figure 8.7 is faded so you can clearly see the lines I painted to show relative sizes and positions of key points on the pose. I used a thin Pens variant with the Straight Line Strokes option in the Property Bar. (Holding down the Shift key constrains your lines to perfect horizontal or vertical.) This version is available in the Lesson 8 folder on the CD for reference. The spaces between horizontal red lines are head measurements. So in this pose, Roz is just under seven heads high. The vertical lines show how various body points line up, and the angled lines give additional guides for checking accuracy. You might want to print the original GypsyRoz14.jpg on a letter-sized page and add your own guide-lines and angles. We will examine this image often as we work.

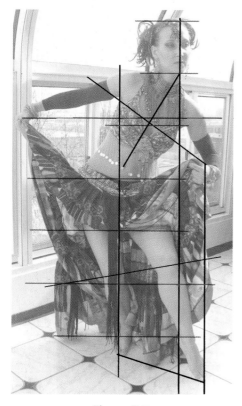

Figure 8.7
Gypsy grid.

Rule of Thumb

In a traditional setting, the artist makes comparative measurements by sighting along his outstretched hand, using a pencil or the thumb. Let's say the model's head is one thumb length. How many thumb lengths is it to her elbow or knee?

Recall working on tinted paper with dark lines for modeling shadow areas and white for picking out highlights (a pear in Lesson 2 and a portrait in Lesson 5)? That technique is great for figures as well as faces and fruit. Choose a medium gray color for the canvas and pull a few dry media variants into a custom palette. Pastels, Charcoal, or Conte sticks, in any combination, are fine. Don't forget to include a Blender or two for softening and smearing edges and wiping out areas that need fixing. You can import my Figure Drawing palette with the Custom Palette Organizer. It has only two items, Tapered Conte 15 and Pointed Stump 20. Feel free to add more brushes to it as you work, but these are enough for starters. The first stage, in Figure 8.8, was done with a few preliminary black strokes with the Conte stick and quite a bit of smearing with the stump. Sure, there's a lot wrong with it (head too big, shoulders too narrow, and so on), but we have to start somewhere.

Is the figure where you want it on the page? When working digitally, you can move the entire image up, down, or sideways and even add extra paper to the edges! It's not necessary to include the entire figure in the drawing, but it is important that the composition be satisfying. That often means having the pose go out past at least one edge of the paper. I like that her outstretched arm shoots out over the edge (that hand would be hard to draw, anyway). But I'll move the entire image up a bit so her foot doesn't hit the edge of the page.

Figure 8.8
First things first.

Figure 8.9 shows some progress. Head and shoulders are in proportion, and most of the parts are lining up the way they should. Notice the model's nose lines up vertically with her left armpit, knee, and heel. Check other vertical line-ups and angles. I've introduced some lighter gray for the negative shapes between her arms and torso. Drawing these shapes correctly will help our accuracy. The lower part of my drawing is still out of whack. Are the legs too short? Is the torso too long? The feet are not at the correct angle relative to each other. I'll change to different shades of gray by accessing the eyedropper as I draw and redraw with the Conte stick.

The stage shown in Figure 8.10 is looking much better, and I feel like the hardest part is over. Proportions are working, and tonal modeling is going well. I've indicated more of the costume and background. Refinements are needed, but I don't want to smooth things out too much. I'd like to keep some of the roughness here and there.

Figure 8.9
Upper-body development.

Figure 8.10
Roughed out.

Switch to a smaller size Conte stick and smudge tool to systematically improve the tonality, adding lighter or darker spots as needed. Details will begin to emerge, but they won't be jumping out quite yet. Tweak for improved accuracy as you go. Hands and feet are challenging, so feel free to leave them less delineated than other parts of the drawing. The focal point is the head and upper body, so they should get more attention. When the drawing is developed to the state shown in Figure 8.11, it's time to decide whether to work on getting a likeness of Roz or allowing it to remain a generic gypsy.

Okay, let's zoom in to about 200 percent and work on the face. Mine will need major reconstructive surgery. But it's all just a collection of shapes, angles, and tonality. Smaller tools are needed, like a 3-pixel Pastel Pencil. The stages in Roz's facial reconstruction are shown in Figure 8.12. The finished Faux Charcoal drawing, with a few splashes of Pastel color, is seen in Figure 8.13.

Figure 8.11
Smoothed out.

Figure 8.12
Face time.

Figure 8.13
Faux finished.

Abstract Painting

The challenge in figure drawing is making your work look like the subject. The challenge in abstract art is making your work NOT look like the subject, or (depending on your definition of abstract) not even having a subject. I'll leave you to explore the history of abstract art movements on your own—Wikipedia would be a good start. You won't need to know anything about specific artists or styles in this section, but it will be helpful to keep a few basic concepts in mind. The essential elements for creating any artwork are the following:

- **Line**: So many possibilities—straight or curved, smooth or jagged, bold or nervous (I could go on).

- **Shape**: Large or small, geometric or organic, simple or complex.

- **Tone (color)**: Dark or light, saturated or dull, warm or cool.

- **Texture**: Rough or smooth, subtle or strong, natural or synthetic.

So there are a lot of choices you can make for each of those four "simple" elements. And the categories can overlap: a line that curves back on itself or is really fat becomes a shape. Lots of lines close together make a texture, and so on. Then you need to work out how to organize them on your canvas. A few principles, in no particular order, will help with that:

- **Contrast**: Not just tonal differences, but contrast in size or complexity of elements creates visual interest.

- **Repetition**: Create unity by repeating some of the elements, with variation in size, color, or angle.

- **Balance**: Composition, or placement of elements so that they work well within the picture plane.

- **Focal point**: Create at least one center of interest so it's not just wallpaper.

Crop and Flop Method

Begin with an existing image—just about any image will do. You'll cut it apart, repeat some of the elements as layers, apply some painted strokes and effects, and with a little inspiration and a "happy accident" or two, you'll get abstract art.

Take another look at the scribble sampler way back at the beginning of Lesson 1. It's not really art and wasn't meant to be, but it's a great resource for experimenting with this approach. I cropped it down to the small section shown in Figure 8.14. Those fluffy pink strokes were made with Bristle Oils (in the Oils category), and the brown scribbles came from a Grainy Pencil. Actually, this already looks very good. There is repetition in having two horizontal bands and in the kind of overlapping strokes used in each area. There is also contrast between the brush strokes and pencil marks. No focal point, yet. Let's see what we can do to make this image swatch more interesting.

Figure 8.14
First you crop.

I made uneven rectangular selections and applied one or two Orientation effects to each one, either Distort or Flip Vertical. Each slice automatically created its own layer so that they could be moved around, overlapped, and the composite method could be changed. For two of the sections, I used Effects > Objects > Create Drop Shadow. The result is shown in Figure 8.15, and the layered RIFF file is available in the Lesson 8 folder for examination and additional manipulation.

Figure 8.15
Flip-flopper.

There is a 3D effect now, resulting from the shadows and overlaps. The irregular edges are much more interesting than the simple strips. Is there a focal point? My eye is attracted to the strong vertical strip that has darker pinks, thanks to Gel mode. That area also includes an important angle (in contrast to the predominant horizontals and verticals), emphasized by a drop shadow. I'm satisfied with these few changes, and I'm not going to force any additional painting or effects (maybe later). If this image were three or four feet wide instead of just a couple of inches, it could easily be hanging in a corporate corridor or upscale hotel. Sometimes it's just that easy.

Variations on a Theme

This time we'll start with a photo. There are several images in the Things folder on the CD that are nearly abstract already, so it will be like "painting fish in a barrel," if you get my drift. I put about a dozen of them into a folder called Abstract This!

The goal will be to create a painting that refers to the subject of the photo and borrows freely from its visual elements, but goes off in its own direction. I'll work with the photo of a wall display of Crocs shoes, shown in Figure 8.16. The colors are gorgeous, and there is a repetition of interesting shapes. I like the clusters of black dots, and my cartoonist mind is seeing some fish-like creatures with their mouths open. I do not have a clear idea where I want to go with this, and I'm rather vague about how to get there. Follow along with me, or do your own thing.

Figure 8.16
That's a Croc!

Basic preparation for any project that begins with a source photo should start with File > Clone. That gives you the original to refer to as you work. It also provides a safety net, enabling you to bring back any of the original areas with a Cloners variant or a brush using Clone Color. It's a good idea to make a New Color Set from Image for easy access to the original colors.

I really like those dot clusters, and I want to make a brush that will allow me to rubber stamp them in various sizes and colors. Refer to Figure 8.17 for the steps I used to create a CrocsDot variant in the Pens category.

First I made a Lasso selection around a group of dots with high contrast. I copied it and used the Paste Into New Image command. I selected the yellow areas around the dots with the Magic Wand and deleted them, leaving me with a bunch of skimpy orange dots. How can we make them black and beef them up? (I'd ask you to scroll down to the answer, but that would just waste paper, so I'll tell you how I did it.) Recall the Woodcut effect in the Surface Control menu. It has a Black Output option, with a few sliders for adjusting heaviness and other qualities.

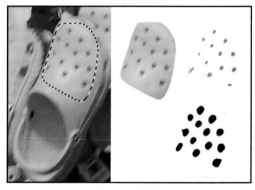

Figure 8.17
Dots o' Croc!

One more step remains, and that's to turn the black dots into a captured Dab. First choose a variant that already has the qualities you want (a solid opaque look) with no paper grain. I chose the Flat Color variant in the Pens group. Now make a rectangular selection around the group of dots and use the Capture Dab command at the top of the Brush Selector Bar popup menu. Give this new variant a name with the Save Variant command. (Don't forget to restore default settings to the Flat Color brush.) Like its "parent," this new variant does not produce size changes in response to pressure, so I'll need to use the Size slider in the Property Bar for major size adjustments or use bracket keys for minor changes. I could designate pressure as an input variable using the Size section in the Brush Controls.

As with the Crop 'n' Flop project, we need a focal point to avoid the "wallpaper" look of a repeating pattern. The yellow shoes are marginally brighter than the rest of the image, so let's push for more contrast. There are numerous ways to do that. Using Layer Masks seems a good choice because we haven't worked with them yet.

We'll need to put a another copy of the cloned canvas image on its own layer. Selecting Edit > Copy followed by Edit > Paste in Place will do that. To desaturate the layer (that is, remove all color), use Effects > Tonal Control > Adjust Colors and move the Saturation slider all the way to the left.

At this point, your Layers Palette should look like Figure 8.18; your working image is in grays because it is 100% opaque in Default mode. You can change the composite method to alter the relation-ship between the layers, but what you want in this case is to have a bright and highly saturated area around the yellow shoes, fading to less saturation as you go to the edges of the image. A Layer Mask will be necessary to accomplish that.

Painting versus Photoshopping

If you're fortunate enough to own both Painter and Photoshop, feel free to do image manipulation maneuvers in either program. They are more compatible than ever; just use the PSD (Photoshop Document) format for layered files, as they can be opened in Painter. Photoshop does not recognize RIFF files, however. Incidentally, Adobe hates it when you use "photoshop" as a verb.

Create Layer Mask

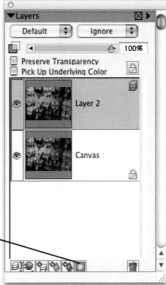

Figure 8.18
Layers of shoes.

Click on the Create Layer Mask icon. A blank white rectangle appears next to the image thumbnail on your Layers Palette. The Layer Mask determines the visibility of pixels in the layer, or how much the canvas beneath will show through. White is fully opaque, black is 100 percent transparent, and shades of gray will produce partial visibility. So if you paint with black or gray on that Layer Mask, corresponding parts of the layer will disappear or fade. This is non-destructive, and painting with white makes those pixels visible again. Applying a two-point gradient from black to white will create a smooth transition from transparency to opacity, and that's what we'll do.

If you want to change the way black blends into white, use the Edit Gradient command in the Gradients Palette popup menu. The Edit Gradient dialog box, shown in Figure 8.19, has a color ramp bar (grayscale in this case) with control points along its bottom edge. To change the point where black and white transition, click on the ramp to create a new control point and move it toward the black end. This will make for a faster change from black to white, concentrating the transparent effect at the point where you click the Paint Bucket on the Layer Mask. Be sure to click on the pixels corresponding to the center of the bright yellow shoes.

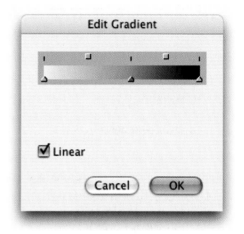

Figure 8.19
Ramping up.

Figure 8.20 shows the Gradients Palette after editing (angle doesn't matter because we're using the radial style), and Figure 8.21 shows how the Layer Mask looks after the gradient has been applied. That black center will produce complete transparency, allowing the highly saturated color of the canvas image to be at full strength.

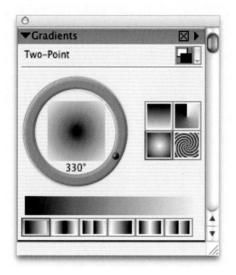

Figure 8.20
Two-point radial gradient.

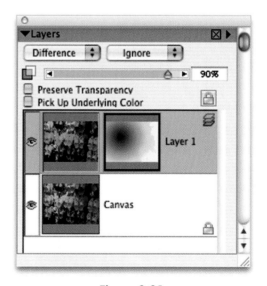

Figure 8.21
Gradual mask.

Head for the Border

A black border around the mask thumbnail indicates that it is active. If you want to work on the image layer instead of the mask, click on its thumbnail.

The result wasn't that interesting. But a little experimenting with composite methods made all the difference, literally. I switched to Difference mode and reduced opacity of the layer to 90 percent for the effect in Figure 8.22. Now, instead of gradual reduction in saturation, I get gradual darkening toward the edges, with some color changes—unplanned, unexpected, and totally acceptable.

Figure 8.22
Making a difference.

Save this version and drop the layer into the canvas to prepare for some actual painting! Well, smearing, at least for now. Several brushes can help make the shoes less recognizable, in a painterly style. Variants from the Blender and Palette Knife categories are possible choices. Smeary Varnish from the Impasto group will add thick paint to your smears. Let's try all three. Make a custom palette containing these items:

- Blender > Pointed Stump 20

- Palette Knife > Palette Knife (from the Department of Redundancy Department)

- Impasto > Smeary Varnish

Make a clone copy of this version, if you want a safety net again. Now you can enjoy the "smear without fear" experience. Use any combination of smeary tools to obliterate detail, including the dots— remember, we made a special brush to create dot clusters whenever we need them. The Palette Knife will need to be reduced in size for better control. And you might want to save that smaller version as its own custom variant. When using Smeary Varnish, work at 100% magnification, or the Depth effect won't look right. As you work to minimize the "shoeness" of the image, keep visual interest high with variation in texture and by using strokes that follow the contours of the shapes (always good advice). Figure 8.23 has a reasonable amount of smearing for this stage.

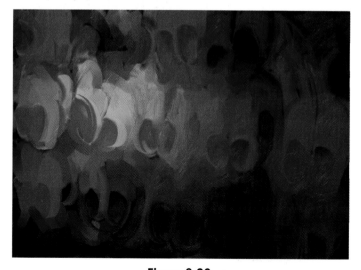

Figure 8.23

Footwear wearing down.

In the service of repetition, let's paint in some variations of those oval "fish-mouth" shapes, using RealBristle Brushes (version X) or Artists Oils. Both of those brush categories are capable of painting with more than one color at a time. You'll need the Color Mixer to load these brushes with multiple colors. (Review Lesson 5 for Mixer basics.) Create a Mixer Pad with the major colors from the image blending roughly into each other so you can sample them with the multi-color eyedropper. For your convenience there is a Mixer Pad called Crocs Shoes in the Palettes and Libs folder on the CD, looking like Figure 8.24. Open it from the Mixer popup menu.

I painted some curves and arcs with Real Oils Short and really like the results. This stage is shown in Figure 8.25, and I think you'll agree this is no longer just a collection of silly looking shoes. I'm tempted to consider it done, but I still haven't used my CrocsDots brush. This would be a good time to try it.

Figure 8.24
Shoe pad.

Figure 8.25
You don't look shoe-ish!

I stamped out several dot clusters in different colors and sizes, including one set on the yellow "source" shoe, bringing back the original reference. A bit of smudging was applied here and there with the Blender stump. The right side of the image has more detail now, as you can see in Figure 8.26. This version is more playful and seems a bit frilly, but I still have the previous "butch" version. Both of them are solutions to the challenge of creating an abstract painting from a realistic photo. The ongoing challenge in fine art is to know when you're done.

Figure 8.26
I'll take yellow in a size 7.

What's Next?

Congratulations on making it through a very intense lesson requiring you to stretch your skills and imagination. I invite you to come back and repeat some of these projects again with different source images. Take your best paintings from this session and print them on canvas or watercolor paper specially made for desktop inkjet printers. If you want to produce large output, see the "Resources" section in the Appendix.

And now, for something completely different—in the next lesson, you'll become an animator.

9 Pixel-Based Animation

You've seen the incredible power that Corel Painter has for imitating traditional drawing and painting media. It shouldn't astonish you that Painter can also imitate traditional animation. I'm referring to the time-honored techniques that required drawing and painting by hand on transparent sheets of acetate, or *cels*, which were then photographed by a special camera. Even a short cartoon created in this way can involve teams of specialists for preliminary storyboarding, character design, pencil testing, "tweening" (the job of "inbetweener" involves creating all the frames needed between key frames), inking and painting—well, you get the idea.

On a much smaller scale, you can do all of that using Painter's frame stacks. The "onion skin" feature serves the function of cels, allowing you to see two or more frames at a time so you can manage the necessary amount of change between frames. That's the essence of animation—creating a series of images with slight changes between them so that a rapid viewing of the sequence fools the eye into seeing movement.

You'll be happy to know there are shortcuts and ways to automate some of the work to take a lot of tedious repetition off your hands. Also, there are many styles of experimental animation (without cartoon characters!) that can be created quickly. When you're done, you can save your frame stack in a variety of video or movie formats, including GIF animations for the Web.

Digital Cel Basics

Let's set up a blank frame stack and make a quick animation of a worm crossing from one edge of the frame to the other. (The process will be quick, but the worm can travel at various speeds.) Choose File > New and enter a convenient size, say 7 inches wide by 5 inches high (or whatever it is in the metric system for the rest of the civilized world), at screen resolution 72 ppi, and choose a paper color other than white; but don't click OK yet. Notice the Movie option at the bottom of the dialog box. Click on the Movie button and enter **10** in the Frames field for a very short movie. When you click OK, you'll be prompted to name your movie and decide where to put it. With that handled, one more decision is presented: how many layers of onion skin do you want? Accept the default minimum of 2 and the default storage type.

Finally, Painter will create the 10-frame stack to your specifications, and the Frame Stacks Palette will appear. You'll use this to navigate between frames and (with the Playback slider) determine the speed of the animation in frames per second (fps). That handy frame-rate control was introduced in Painter IX. Figure 9.1 displays the Frame Stacks Palette with two frames visible at once, because we chose 2 layers of onion skin. All frames have the blue paper color I chose. Frame 1 is ready for you to work on, as indicated by the red triangle above it.

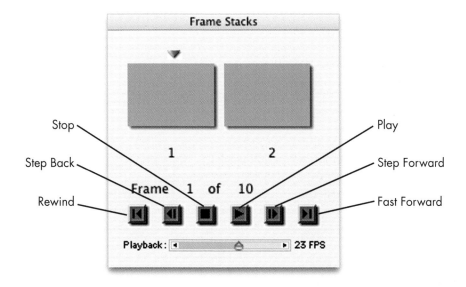

Figure 9.1
Short stack.

Start with a Worm

What brush variants are good for drawing a worm? How about the Gradient Repeat Pen? The Furry Brush from the F-X category (maybe with a size reduction)? I'll use the Barbed Wire Pen. Make some practice strokes on frame 1, and customize your brush as desired. Then delete or undo your test strokes in the usual way, or use the Erase Frame command in the Movie menu.

You Have Been Erased!

The Erase Frame command removes all marks and restores a fresh background (paper color) to the frame, but Delete Frame removes the frame from the stack altogether, reducing the total number of frames.

Let's plunge right in, without any planning—my favorite approach to most projects. Well, maybe a very simple plan: make the worm enter on the left and exit at the right. So the first stroke on frame 1 is just a little bit of the worm's "head" poking out from the edge of the frame. Step forward to frame 2 and turn on Tracing Paper, either by clicking its icon at the upper right edge of your image window or using Cmd/Ctrl+T. Now you can see the slightly less opaque Onion Skin image from frame 1 to use as a reference for the next brush stroke. Make that second stroke overlapping the first one but coming out into the frame a bit more. You'll be estimating how much overlap there should be between strokes in order to come out at the right edge in frame 10. If your worm gets to the right edge before the end of the movie, you can eliminate the empty frames with the Delete Frames command in the Movie menu. If your worm can't make it to the finish line in 10 frames, make additional blank frames by simply clicking the Step Forward button on the Frame Stacks Palette.

Make the worm wiggle across the frame by giving each brush stroke a slight curve, and alternate the direction of the curves from one frame to the next. Figure 9.2 shows my frame stack with frame 8 active and tracing paper on, so both frame 8 and the previous frame are visible. Play the movie at any point while you're working so you can check for any problems (like an early bird waiting to swoop down for a fuzzy snack). Notice that the movie automatically loops over and over, so the worm will keep reappearing at the left edge and tirelessly make his way offstage again and again. My wiggly worm is available for you to examine or edit in the Lesson 9 folder on the CD. There are several other Painter movies there to demonstrate other projects in this lesson, or just for fun.

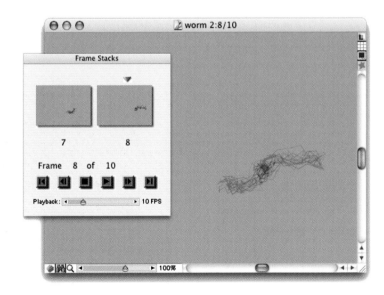

Figure 9.2

Maybe it's a caterpillar.

You Can Play That Again!

Painter movies are automatically saved as frame stacks, uncompressed files that can get huge in a hurry. Our one-second worm is a 7MB file, so a one-minute movie with the same frame dimensions would be (let's see now) 420 MB! You'll want to use Save As options: QuickTime (on the Mac platform) and AVI (for the PC) are formats that enable viewing your movies with your favorite player utility. The files can be compressed enough to share with friends via e-mail attachments. With the compression settings I chose, that 7MB worm got trimmed down to a petite 32 KB.

After this quick-n-dirty trial run, you can imagine the potential for creating longer frame stacks with more complex drawings and multiple layers of onion skin for better control over your animated elements. Hang onto that worm movie, in case you want to enhance it later: add a sunrise, a scrolling background, or another critter.

Automating Animating

If that exercise wasn't quick and easy enough for you, here's a labor saving technique that will allow you to sit back and let Painter divide a brush stroke into the number of frames you want. Just two commands are needed: Record Stroke in the Brush Selector Bar popup menu and Apply Brush Stroke to Movie in the Movie menu.

Just add this effect to your worm movie. See, I knew it would come in handy again. Be sure to use the Record Stroke command before you make the stroke. I switched to blue for my new worm, and Figure 9.3 shows the brush stroke that's about to be animated. I painted it from right to left, so it will cross the frame in the opposite direction. Yes, the stroke was made on one of the frames of my movie, for convenience, but the Undo command got rid of it. This had no effect on the recording function.

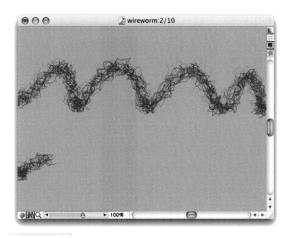

Figure 9.3

The worm turns.

No Turning Back

Changes to a movie can't be undone. Before adding another element to your movie, save it in QuickTime or AVI format, then reopen it and give it a different name. It will expand to a frame stack again, and the original version will be protected. Also be advised that while you work on a movie, there's no Undo available for a frame after you've advanced to another frame.

When the Apply Brush Stroke to Movie command is chosen, my fancy barbed wire stroke becomes a madly bouncing worm rushing past the little red wriggler. Check it out by playing the 2wireworms frame stack.

There's another way to animate a brush stroke that gives you much more control. Right under the Record Stroke command is Playback Stroke. This feature lets you repeat a recorded stroke with a single tap of your Wacom pen (or click of your mouse). Playback can save time spent redoing the same stroke frame after frame if the only thing that needs changing is its position. There are some other clever ways to use this feature, such as changing colors and even switching to a different brush variant between taps. To see various ways a single oval stroke can be played back, see Figure 9.4. Can you recognize all the variants used? That smeary effect on the right comes from Coarse Distorto in the Distortion category, and the distressed area in the center is the work of Impasto > Acid Etch. Image Hose sprayed the gardenias in the lower left corner, and Pattern Pen Masked was used with both Double Helix and Silver Tubing. Not a bad way to create an abstract painting, actually.

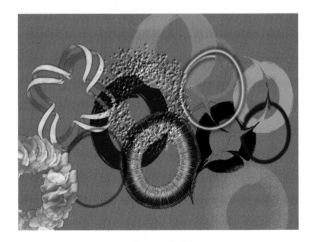

Figure 9.4

Please repeat that.

Make another frame stack with the same dimensions as before and a dark background color. You don't have to know how many frames you'll need. You can start with just one, and every time you use the Step Forward button, you'll get a new frame. This time choose three levels of onion skin. We'll create a short abstract movie using the Playback Stroke feature. Choose Record Stroke again and make a scribble or shape on the first frame using any brush variant you like and undo it. Now engage the Playback Stroke function and turn on tracing paper. Make the scribble move smoothly or change its acceleration. With three levels of onion skin, it's easier to plan the speed of your scribble across the screen. Between each frame, you'll change colors and/or variants. Experiment with some of the wilder brushes to make your movie more exciting. Hey, with no budget, no stars, and no plot, we've gotta try anything!

Figure 9.5 shows the stroke I recorded. On a dark background, light colors will show up well, as long as the brush variants use Cover mode. My abstract sunrise took 13 frames. I named the movie Sunrise Playback, with reference to the technique. You'll find it for viewing in the Lesson 9 folder on the CD. Figure 9.6 shows a frame with tracing paper on so that two previous frames are visible. Those three frames are also showing in the Frame Stacks Palette.

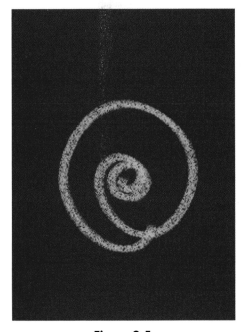

Figure 9.5

Recorded spiral.

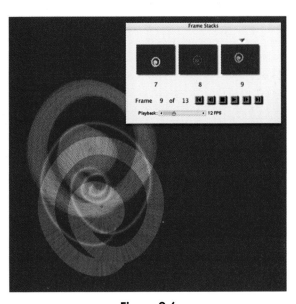

Figure 9.6

Onion skinning.

Your Files Are Numbered

Around the time I was preparing the screen shot for Figure 9.6, I realized that my frame dimensions were twice as big as I wanted them to be. There's no way to resize movie frames while you're working on the frame stack, but there's a workaround. One of the options in File > Save As is Save the Movie As Numbered Files. When this is chosen, Painter will create a standard RIFF file for each frame. When you're prompted to name the sequence, be sure to include "01" or "001" (to accommodate the total number of frames) at the beginning or the end of the file name. Painter will automatically number the remaining frames. I had to open all 13 files and resize each one. Imagine how tedious that can be if you have 50 or 100 files to fix! So as the carpenters say, "Measure twice, cut once."

Working with Layers

If you want to animate an image element that's more complex than a single stroke, create it first or select it from a source image and drag it onto your first movie frame. It will become a layer and can be manipulated like any other layer. Scale it, rotate it, distort it, adjust the colors, or apply any effects you like. When you step forward to the next frame, the layer is merged into the canvas in the previous frame but available for any adjustments in the current frame. Continue from one frame to the next. Be sure to deselect the layer in the final frame.

I grabbed a tomato slice from the Image Portfolio and made it fly off into space by using the Effects/Scale command and typing in the percentage of size reduction for each position change. (Need a reminder about the Image Portfolio? Look at Lesson 7 again.) My stack of tomato slices can be viewed and edited or tossed with a nice vinaigrette. The eight frames were saved as numbered files in a folder named Flying Tomato Files in the Lesson 9 folder on the CD.

Stack 'Em Up

Here's how to open numbered files as a frame stack. Choose File > Open and check the Open Numbered Files box near the bottom. You'll be prompted to choose the first file in a sequence and then the last file. You'll have to give the frame stack a name. Be sure the file name is unique to protect other movies you may be working on.

I took my own advice, for a change, and saved the tomato movie before adding a background. I chose the aptly named Red Streak gradient for a background fill. I made the background animate by changing its angle in the Gradients Palette with each frame, moving the red button on the Angle Ring clockwise. Figure 9.7 shows the Gradients Palette, and Figure 9.8 has two frames with Onion Skin turned on. The result was a tomato slice flying through a turning spiral. Play the Tomato Escapes frame stack, also available in the Lesson 9 folder. It's not bad, considering the few frames involved and my casual attitude about accurate placement.

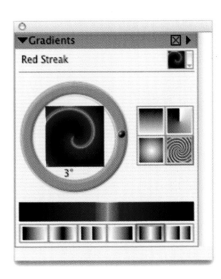

Figure 9.7

Know the angles.

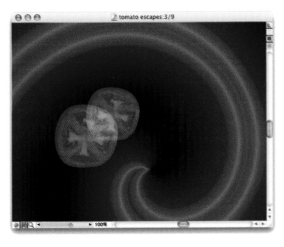

Figure 9.8

Flying tomato.

Movie Scripts

This has nothing to do with adding dialogue—Painter has no sound capability at all. I'm referring to Painter's system for recording a sequence of brush strokes and/or effects for playback on a blank or existing image. When you press the red button on the Scripts Palette, shown in Figure 9.9, everything you do is recorded until you press the Stop button. Give the script a name, and it will be added to your Scripts library. To play a script, use the Playback Script command in the Scripts menu. To apply a script automatically to an entire frame stack, you need the Apply Script to Movie command in the Movie menu.

Keeping Records

Record and play back the script for an entire painting to have a review of your creative process, as all your undos and changes are part of the action. This makes a great demonstration or teaching aid. (Yes, I'm kicking myself for not recording the GypsyRoz drawing in Lesson 8!) The appearance of brush strokes quickly one after another makes an interesting kind of animation, too.

Figure 9.9
We are recording.

Royalty-Free Characters

My favorite sources for "artsy" animation are the stopped motion photography of E. Muybridge, who—in the 1870s before the advent of motion pictures—devised a way to create a series of still photographs of animals and people in action. Figure 9.10 shows a sample of Muybridge's remarkable work. Several sets of his photos are available to you in the Lesson 9 folder on the CD. They just need to be opened as numbered files. No worries about copyright infringement after 130 years!

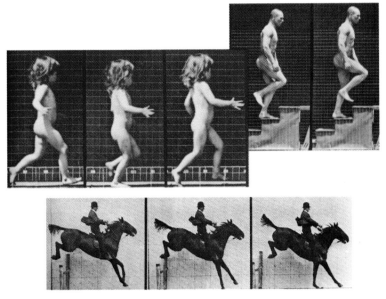

Figure 9.10
Muybridge action photos.

Let's create a script for adding color to a Muybridge frame stack. (There was no color film in 1870!) Open the MuyDancer source movie by double-clicking the frame stack or opening the numbered files. A great way to add exciting colors to a grayscale image instantly (my favorite speed) is to apply the colors from a gradient preset. Look at the choices in the Gradient library and find one you like. I picked Vivid Mixture. Engage the record function (red button) on the Scripts Palette. Now use the Express in Image command from the Gradient popup menu on any frame in the stack. This brings up a Bias slider and a preview so you can determine how you want the gradient colors mapped to the luminosity (values) of the image. Figure 9.11 shows the slider position that makes a pleasing color map in my opinion. If you like the result, stop recording and give the script a name. I called mine Xpress Grad. If you don't like the result, stop recording and press Cancel. Try again with a different gradient or bias setting. It's a good idea to Undo the action(s) on the frame to return it to the original state before you continue working.

Figure 9.11
Vivid color mapping.

Choose Movie > Apply Script to Movie and select your new script for playback. Sit back and watch each frame get the color treatment. For long movies and complex scripts, you can take a leisurely lunch or coffee break. Play your new version of the movie. Be sure to save it in QuickTime or AVI format before you continue working.

Smudge-o-matic

Try making a script with multiple brush strokes. Smudging and smearing can be used to get painterly effects, especially with bristly variants like Smeary Varnish from the Impasto category. But if you make a script using smeary strokes on the figure in one frame, those same strokes won't match the figure on other frames. You just might have to smear the dancer by hand in each frame. But there is a way to automate smearing of the background in each frame. Consider recording all the brush strokes needed to make a complete smeary painting on a frame that you have saved as an image, without special attention to the particular pose of the dancer. Save it as a script. Now, instead of using Apply Script to Movie, we'll use the Playback Script function on each frame individually. Prepare each frame by making a rough Lasso selection around the figure and inversing the selection so that only the background will be affected by the script. Figure 9.12 shows the end result of smearing all over the image with a Pointed Stump from the Blender variants.

Figure 9.12
Fits into the abstract lesson, too.

The woman in Figure 9.13 is surrounded by a loose Lasso selection. Don't spend much time trying to be accurate—the whole idea here is to save time. At this point, you'll either choose Select > Invert or use the Draw Outside option at the lower left of your image window. Use the Playback command on the Scripts Palette and choose your smeary script. Figure 9.14 shows a different frame after the smeary background has been done.

Draw inside
Draw outside
Draw anywhere

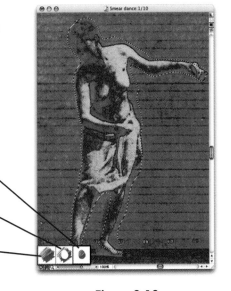

Figure 9.13
Get these marching ants off me!

Figure 9.14
Smeared background.

The next stage involves smudging each figure by hand, using painterly strokes with your favorite smeary tools. My results are shown in the illustration at the beginning of the lesson. As a test, I did one frame without automating the smears at all. Figure 9.15 was done mostly with Smeary Varnish and a few Pointed Stump strokes. The style is reminiscent of Paul Gauguin (Van Gogh's buddy). This lady was just the right age to be Gauguin's girlfriend!

Figure 9.15
Post-impressionist flavor.

Not Everything Can Be Scripted.

I wanted to change the dancer's vivid colors to muted tones using Color Scheme options in the Underpainting Palette. The Sketchbook Color Scheme looked lovely, as does Classical, but they must be applied "by hand" to each frame. Here's a workaround: apply the Color Scheme you like to one frame and make a New Color Set From Image. Now use Effects > Tonal Control > Posterize Using Color Set, which is a command that can be made into a script. This script will use whatever color set is current.

Rotoscope Cloning

Traditional *rotoscoping* is a way to project a single frame from live action footage in perfect alignment with the animator's drawing surface. The animator draws each cel based on the action of the figure in the projected frame, then steps forward to the next frame in the action to draw on the next cel. The classic example is Disney's dancing hippos in the 1940s film *Fantasia*. A real ballerina was filmed dancing, and the footage was projected one frame at a time so the cartoon hippo's actions could be more realistic. It's all about the action, not necessarily recreating the original figure.

Corel Painter can function as a digital rotoscope! It's just a matter of finding suitable movie (or video) sources or sequences of still images that create action when they are viewed quickly enough. The Muybridge action photos are a great resource, once again. The Lesson 9 folder includes horses jumping, a kid running, and a guy climbing stairs.

Keep Dancing

The basis for rotoscoping in Painter is establishing a frame-by-frame connection between a source frame stack and a destination frame stack. Both stacks must have the same dimensions and number of frames. Let's continue working with the dancer. Use either your color version or the original grayscale sequence. You'll be designating this stack as the clone source and using the Tracing Paper feature to guide your work on the blank frames. Recall that Painter X provides adjustable opacity for tracing paper.

Drawing a Blank?

Your destination stack doesn't have to be blank, of course. It can be another movie or a video clip. It's possible to add an animated element to a live action scene, a prepared background, or other rotoscoped images.

Before we jump in, let's consider enlarging the frame size and resolution of the source images. Way back in Lesson 5, you were given an exception to the rule against "sampling up" (increasing the resolution of an image without improving quality), but it's worth repeating.

You Can Say That Again!

If you have a small and/or low-resolution image to use as a clone source for a drawing or painting, increase the resolution as much as you like *before* you create the clone copy. Your brush strokes will be at the higher resolution.

I'm going to make the dancer frames bigger. We need the pixel dimensions of those dancer frames, but the Resize command is grayed out. If you didn't notice those numbers before, here's a way to get that info. With any frame active (they're all the same size), choose Select > All followed by Edit > Copy, then Edit > Paste Into New Image. Now you can use the Resize command to find out the height and width of the new image. Select File > New and enter those dimensions. Be sure to choose the Movie option and enter the number of frames needed. In this case, it's 10. Before you click OK, choose a paper color for the background. I picked a mauve-pink.

Click on the source movie again to make it active and choose Set Move Clone Source from the Movie menu. Now make the blank stack active and turn on tracing paper. You should see the ghost image of frame 1 on your blank frame 1. When you step forward, the ghost image will change to the corresponding frame in the source. You're good to go! Use any brush variant or style you like. Possibilities include the following:

- Accurate outline of the figure with a fine-point pen or pencil.

- Sketchy gesture with a larger variant, such as Conte sticks or oil pastels.

- Painting with one or more Cloner variants (or any brush using Clone Color).

- Filling the shape of the figure with scribbles, using the Nervous Pen or other quirky variants.

There are samples of most of those techniques in Figure 9.16. The dancer frame (in another color scheme) was made with the Fine Spray Cloner. The little girl running sequence began with an Express Gradient in Image script applied, then I did several versions, two of which are shown here. The full frame was done with Grainy Water smudging and strokes with the Marbling Rake from the Distortion category—no cloning involved, just working directly on the colorized frame stack, as we did with the dancer. The little girl on a white background was made with the Van Gogh Cloner. I had a lot of fun scribbling with the Nervous Pen on the jumping horse sequence. As for the other two horses, I wish I could remember how I did those. If you can figure it out, let me know. I might want to do it again.

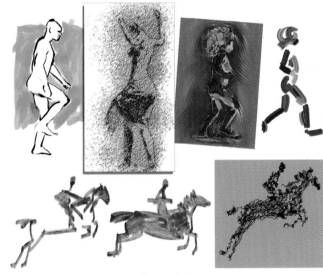

Figure 9.16
Muy techniques.

Goghing, Going, Gone!

Take another look at the Van Gogh clone of the little girl running. This was done in Painter 8 (or earlier) when the Van Gogh Cloner behaved differently: the color of the pixel you started with remained for the entire stroke, forcing you to make lots of short strokes (ideally following the shapes in the image). The Van Gogh Cloner in versions IX and X produces strokes that continually update color information from the clone source. The result is not nearly as (um) con-vince-ing.

To get more ideas, play the frame stacks of Muybridge rotoscopes I've created over the years using different versions of Painter. Feel free to use a combination of techniques. Consider using different brushes and styles from one frame to the next—a great method for those of us who have a hard time making decisions. I encourage you, as always, to experiment.

Dancing Backwards

Okay, enough discussion. Let's rotoscope this lady. You may have a problem when you finish frame 1 and step forward to frame 2. With tracing paper on, you are seeing not only the source frame, but also the work you just did on frame 1. Seeing your work on the previous frame or two is essential if you're creating from scratch, but now it's just getting in the way. What to do? The solution is so simple you've probably thought of it already.

Yes, work backwards! If you start on frame 10, there's nothing in frame 9 to intrude. So keep going back a frame at a time and stop when you get to the beginning! Figure 9.17 has some frames from the rotoscoped dancer showing a different Cloner variant in each frame. You can play it (and change it); just open the frame stack file MuyDancer XG clone. (The XG stands for Xpress Gradient.)

I quite like the Fiber Cloner effect, shown on the right. At first glance the Fiber Cloner appears to be just a beefy bundle of Nervous Pen strokes with the Value slider in Color Variability controls turned way up. Recall that the Barbed Wire Pen is already a bundle of nerves. Will it create the same look if we enable Clone Color? Let's check it out.

Figure 9.17
Let's do "The Clone!"

These variants are remarkably similar, despite having different Dab Types. They both have a significant amount of Jitter, as you can see in the Random section of Brush Controls, and their tangles tend to straighten out when your stroke speeds up. For the Fiber Cloner, Jitter is expressed by Velocity. In Figure 9.18, the fiber stroke on the extreme left starts slowly at the top, speeds up considerably, and then slows down again at the bottom. At top speed, the lines are straight and parallel, like a Rake stroke. The Barbed Wire Pen never straightens out completely, as shown in the center stroke, which was drawn very quickly. The remaining strokes were made with Barbed Wire using Clone Color. We see the result of dragging more slowly, then increasing size from 7 pixels to 12, and the last stroke was made with Value variability at 45%. Both of these variants can be made to spew vast quantities of fiber, even while your pen isn't moving, by enabling Continuous Time Deposition in the Spacing controls. That's how the blob at the top was made, with my stylus held in one place.

Figure 9.18
You need more fiber.

189

Dance Marathon

Our little 10-frame movie can become more substantial by splicing a number of versions together or adding frame stacks with different actions. The Insert Movie command in the Movie menu offers a way to combine movies having the same frame dimensions. The number of frames doesn't matter. Convert numbered image files or QuickTime or AVI movies to frame stacks again so they can be accessed with the Insert Movie feature. Figure 9.19 shows enough variations on the running girl to turn a 13-frame sprint into a 72-frame marathon lasting nearly a full 5 seconds (at 15fps)!

One of the original source photos is shown along with a couple of treatments you've seen. There's that Fiber Cloner again. The purple, green, and pink figure on a black background was made from the Van Gogh Cloner version (look at Figure 9.16 again). This was accomplished by inverting the colors with Effects > Tonal Control > Negative. Some Glass Distortion was also added, using the Dynamic Plugin Layer by that name. The little pink girl on the brown background was actually drawn with a Pen variant. Once again, the Negative command was invoked on that pink image to make the dark green girl in the last frame. Paper texture was added with Effects > Surface Control > Apply Surface Texture, and a little more Glass Distortion.

Figure 9.19

Keeps going, and going, and...

You Can't Have Everything

All Effects commands, such as Negative and Apply Surface Texture, can be recorded as scripts, and then applied to an entire frame stack. I tried making scripts for Dynamic Plugin Layer effects, with no success.

Let's do a couple more versions before we let this little girl take a much needed rest. (She's been dead for 60 or 70 years, so that's a moot point.) Figure 9.20 shows what you can do with the original grayscale photo when you use Effects > Surface Control > Apply Screen. Remember using this effect on the high-heeled shoe in Lesson 6? You get to choose any three colors and determine how much of the image is filled with each of them, by using Threshold sliders. Figure 9.21 shows the settings I chose. This time Paper is the source for luminosity variation to influence the distribution of colors. Basic Paper works nicely, but you can switch to any paper in your current library while this dialog box is open.

Figure 9.20

Red, white, and blue.

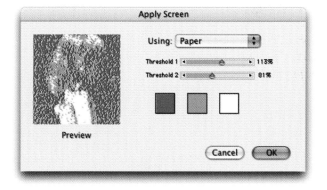

Figure 9.21

Pick a color, any color.

The effect in Figure 9.22 was made on the original photo with an effect in the Esoterica group called Pop Art Fill. The settings are in Figure 9.23. You only get two colors with this effect, and the fill is always dots, imitating the half-tone screens used for offset printing of comic books and pulp magazines in the old days, before digital printing.

Figure 9.22

Call me "Dot."

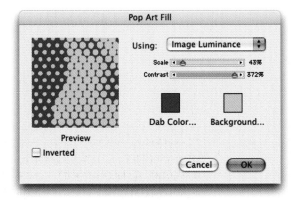

Figure 9.23

Half-tone for a half-pint.

What's Next?

Once again, I've kept my promise to you—I haven't covered everything about this subject! But you don't need much hand holding at this point, and I expect you will continue working on your own. If you like scripted effects you can use the technique with video footage. If rotoscoping turns you on, be advised that all of Muybridge's photo sequences are available for purchase. (See the "Resources" section of the Appendix.) Of course, you can rotoscope other images or movies.

Well, if there's anything important I haven't told you about Painter so far, I better do it in the next lesson.

PAINTBUCKET RESERVOIR
Federal Wetness Protection Program

10 Illustration Projects

What's the difference between fine art and illustration? Fine art hangs on the wall, and illustrations get published. Well, that's the idea, but there's a lot of overlap. If you digitize the *Mona Lisa* and put a pair of jeans on her, you've got an ad. (It's actually been done. Mona's been public domain for even longer than Muybridge photos.) On the other hand, commercial art can hang in a museum after only a few decades. Examples include early 20th century orange crate labels and the psychedelic posters for 1960s rock concerts.

Many of the images you've already created with Painter could be used as illustrations under the right circumstances. In this lesson, you'll work on creating images specifically for publication. These assignments will encourage you to combine a variety of techniques covered in early lessons. But first, let's set some type.

Working with Type

In the world of professional print publishing, a graphic designer will typically use a vector-based program like Illustrator or a page-layout program such as InDesign to create the text needed to accompany your illustration. (It's good to own stock in Adobe Systems.) But if a special effect is desired for a few words or letters, it might be necessary to use a pixel-based program and make it part of your image. Both Painter and Photoshop have terrific, but very different, options for text effects.

P.S, I Love You

Text made with page layout or word processor applications uses Adobe's PostScript technology, allowing crisp high-quality printing at any size (like a vector-based image). Pixel-based programs can only provide bit-map text, which will not look good at small sizes and might even be illegible.

Typography 101

Your Wacom tablet won't be necessary for most of this section, but don't forget where you put it. Even if you know the meaning of "kerning" and can pronounce "leading" correctly, don't skip this part.

Painter's Text tool icon is a capital letter "T." When it is active, the Property Bar gives you many of the standard choices for font, point size, and alignment. In addition to those settings, you can choose to have a drop shadow or an interior shadow applied automatically as you enter text on your canvas. There are separate color and opacity controls, as well as composite method choices for the text and its shadow. Just highlight Text Attributes or Shadow Attributes to alter them independently. Figure 10.1 gets you acquainted with these options.

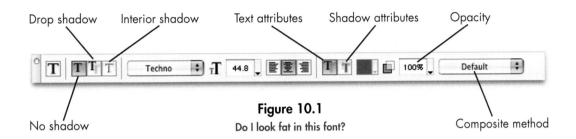

Drop shadow   Interior shadow   Text attributes   Shadow attributes   Opacity

No shadow

Composite method

Figure 10.1
Do I look fat in this font?

Figure 10.2 shows my text in blue with a magenta drop shadow. The variations in Figures 10.3 through 10.5 were made just by playing with shadows, blurs, and composite methods. The figure captions describe how each one was done. Figure 10.5 shows that underlying color can have an influence on the color of the text.

Figure 10.2
Basic blue with a magenta lining.

Figure 10.3
Text uses Reverse-Out method.

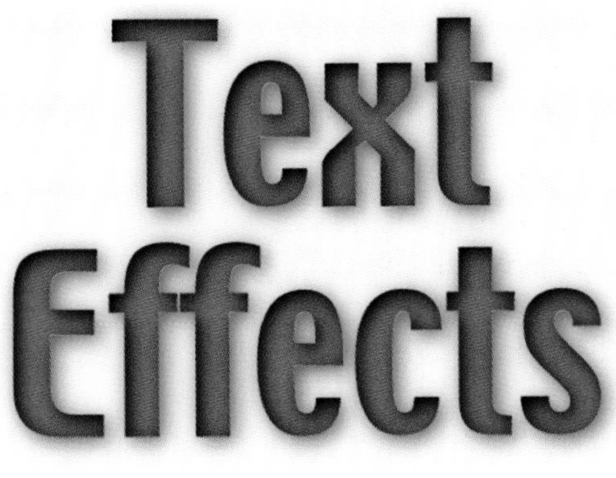

Figure 10.4
Text uses Reverse-Out, shadow is green and blurred.

Figure 10.5
Text in Difference method, shadow using Colorize.

The Text Palette, shown in Figure 10.6, gives you most of the Property Bar choices and more. Here's where you'll adjust tracking (letter spacing) and leading (line spacing) and assign a curve style. There doesn't seem to be a way to kern (fine-tune spacing between two letters).

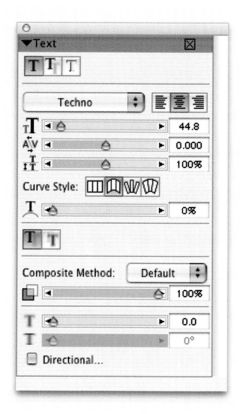

Caution

If you're familiar with Photoshop's nifty Warp Text feature, prepare to be disappointed by Painter's version of text on a curve. There are only three styles, and the curves must be edited with the Shape Selector tool. If you're a skilled manipulator of vector-type anchor points and direction lines, you might be okay.

Figure 10.6
Don't let me catch you kids kerning!

Rasterize Me!

Text occupies its own special layer, clearly marked with the T icon, as shown in Figure 10.7. You can keep going back to change the font and any other text attributes as long as you keep the text in this editable state. When you attempt to apply brush strokes or use any commands outside the Text Palette, Painter will ask if you want to commit the text to an image layer. If you agree, your text is converted to ordinary pixels. That's called *rasterizing*.

We made a chunky chocolate bar in Lesson 7 using two Dynamic Plugin layers in tandem: Tear and Bevel. Similar effects can be applied to letterforms once they are rasterized. This time we'll use Burn and Bevel to transform an ordinary letter into an eroded sculptural piece, evoking an ancient mysterious realm. Game designers might see some possibilities here. Figure 10.8 has the freshly typed letter in a font called Gadget. I chose a rather hefty sans serif typeface, knowing that some destruction would still leave enough of it intact. Follow along using a similar typeface, such as Arial Black, Charcoal, or Futura.

Choose Burn from the Dynamic Plugins at the bottom of your Layers Palette. The settings I used are shown in Figure 10.9 for the effect in Figure 10.10. Your settings may vary, depending on the font you're using.

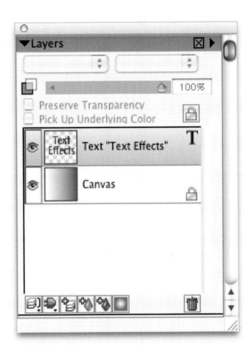

Figure 10.7

I said I'm editable, not edible.

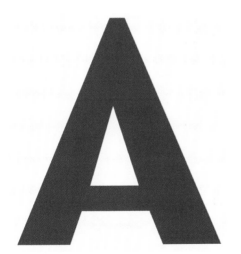

Figure 10.8

A fresh "A."

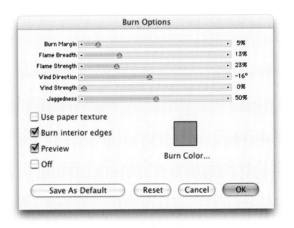

Figure 10.9

Burn, baby, burn!

Refer to the settings in Figure 10.11 for the bevel effect in Figure 10.12. I also added a drop shadow.

Me and My Shadow

You might have noticed that the External Shadow available for text behaves differently from the Drop Shadow you can add to an image layer. A drop shadow exists on its own layer and can be manipulated separately, independent of its more solid counterpart.

Figure 10.10
Jagged and ragged.

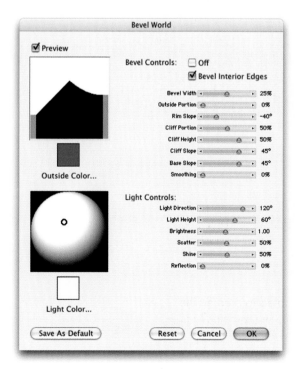

Figure 10.11
Bevel, baby, bevel!

Figure 10.12
Rough and rugged.

When text is rasterized you can paint on it, fill it with a gradient, pattern or texture, push it, pull it, and stomp on it. Some of those options will be inflicted upon the letter "B" for a change. Figure 10.13 shows the before version, and Figure 10.14 demonstrates what can happen when good people use too many effects.

Figure 10.13

Innocent B-standers.

for font freaks

You'll no doubt recognize (from left to right) American Typewriter, Capitals, and Arial Black. Other fonts are fine for the following exercises.

Figure 10.14

F-X frenzy.

I certainly don't want to encourage you to torture type, but I do want to explain the cool techniques used here. The shower door effect on the purple B is the result of applying Effects > Focus > Glass Distortion. I chose to use Basic Paper as the source of luminosity variation.

The B with a cast shadow was more complicated to create. The seashell images look like a Pattern fill, but they were actually made by spraying with the Image Hose. Next, I used Effects > Objects > Drop Shadow. With the letter and its shadow on separate layers, they could be tilted in different directions with Orientation > Distort. Figure 10.15 has part of the Layers Palette with the B and Shadow group open.

Notice there is a Layer Mask on the Shadow layer. It was needed to reduce the opacity of the shadow gradually as it got farther away from the base of the letter. We used a Layer Mask in Lesson 8 to make a gradual transition between two layers. This time the transition is between the shadow and the white canvas. Recall that black areas on a Layer Mask create complete transparency or invisibility for the image on the layer, while white produces 100% opacity, with shades of gray having intermediate effects. A two-point linear gradient was selected using Black and White, with the angle shown in Figure 10.16. Then it was applied to the Layer Mask with the Paint Bucket.

Now we come to the melting, disintegrating letter. First I filled it with Blobs from the Esoterica group in the Effects menu. Yes, the same blobs we used in the Chocolate section of Lesson 7. The real fun begins when you use a Dynamic Plugin called Liquid Lens. You'll need your Wacom tablet for this part. Liquid Lens controls, shown in Figure 10.17, remain open while you work. There are several items for distorting an image in a fluid way. I like the Brush tool for dragging pixels around. That's how the dripping icicles (or whatever) were made. There's no Undo available, but that eraser icon represents a tool for restoring or reverting pixels to their original condition. Partial restoration can produce some intriguing effects. As with all dynamic layers, changes can be made later, and (very important) no harm is being done to the layer beneath. To see what I mean, turn off the visibility of the Liquid Lens layer and you'll see the pristine pre-warp image.

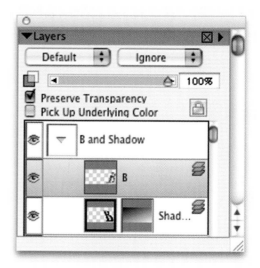

Figure 10.15

B and my shadow.

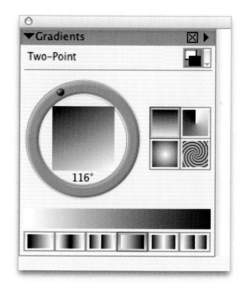

Figure 10.16

That's two points for you.

I prefer using this kind of distortion on faces rather than defenseless members of the alphabet. Try it on images in the People > Heads folder on the CD, members of your family, or high-ranking government officials.

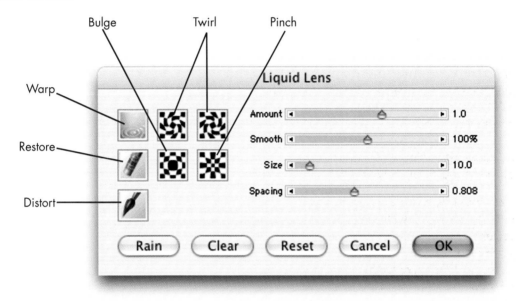

Figure 10.17

The Rain button makes acid rain.

Distortion Is Where You find It

Several of the Liquid Lens tools are similar to variants in the Distortion brush category. Distorto, Pinch, and Bulge are pretty much the same. The Twirl tools are cousins of the Turbulence brush variant. The big difference, of course, is that you can restore pixels selectively only with the dynamic Liquid Lens layer.

Album Cover

Work along with me on a real-world illustration assignment. The client is a jazz pianist and composer who is putting together his first album and commissioned me to create the cover art. I took photographs of Gary playing in a couple of venues. One of those source photos is shown in Figure 10.18. There are several more in the Lesson 10 folder.

Preliminary Sketches

It's customary for an illustrator or designer to make quick "thumbnail" (small) sketches or layouts as the first step. Well, maybe the second step, after a discussion about what the client wants. Digital "sketches" can include quick surface or tonal effects and layered images combined with different composite methods. This part of the process can be fun because your creativity is free to roam. Follow a theme or branch off in another direction, or both. It's so easy to make multiple variations on an image digitally, Just remember to use Iterative Save so the flow of ideas won't be interrupted. And don't overwhelm your client by displaying all the possibilities— just two or three of your best efforts!

Figure 10.18

Jazz man.

The effect in Figure 10.19 begins with a loose Lasso selection of the background. Select > Feather the selection by about 15 pixels for a smooth transition, then use Effects > Focus > Soften for the blur. Invert the selection and apply Effects > Surface Control > Distress using Grain (Paper) to Gary and the piano. I chose Small Dots paper, and I like the crisp black-and-white halftone look, especially in contrast to the soft sepia tones of the blurry background. I had never used the Distress effect before, but it sounded interesting.

Express Texture sounds interesting, too, and it's also in the Surface Control menu. Go back to the original photo and choose Select > All, then Paste in Place to make a copy of the image on its own layer. This step will facilitate the combining of two effects. I applied the Impressionist Color Scheme to the canvas image, then Express Texture using Paper on the layer copy. Figure 10.20 shows the Express Texture dialog with a preview of the Pebble Board effect, a very bold texture that I reduced to about 25% of its scale, using a slider in the Papers Palette. I ended up using Basic Paper instead.

Choosing Screen from the Composite Method list softens the impressionist color scheme and still retains enough grainy texture. This combination appears in Figure 10.21. There are many possible blends of different color schemes with a black-and-white texture, using alternate composite methods. Considering the variety of paper choices available, exploring them could keep you busy for hours.

Figure 10.19
In distress.

Figure 10.20
Grainy Gary.

Figure 10.21
One possible combination.

Figure 10.22 is a pencil drawing made from that source image in Painter, using the classic technique of working on gray paper with dark lines and white highlights. Here are the steps to get you started.

1. Choose medium gray for the main color and use the Set Paper Color command in the Canvas menu.

2. Make a Quick Clone of the photo. The background color will be medium gray.

3. Increase opacity of tracing paper to about 70% (version X) so you see only enough of the source to guide you.

4. Draw with the Cover Pencil or another fine-line pencil or pen that uses the Cover method.

Figure 10.22
Do you take requests?

Head for Cover

Why do we need a Pencil variant using the Cover method for this drawing? Because we want to be able to make white marks on a gray background. Most of the Pencil variants use the Buildup method because that is the way traditional pencils function. You can change the method of any variant in the General section of Brush Controls.

Figure 10.23 has an early stage in this drawing, with an inset showing how the image looks with tracing paper opacity turned up to 80%. You can complete the black line sketch before you add white strokes or switch freely between black and white as you develop the drawing. Although this piece was only an experiment, Gary liked it enough to use it in a performance announcement. The "blues" version is shown at the beginning of the lesson. I added the color using a new layer filled with solid blue, then changed the composite method to Colorize. This kept the white and black untouched and just changed the gray areas.

Figure 10.23
Two pianos, four hands.

An Art Background

The photo in Figure 10.24 has a different look, mainly due to the contrast of the bright abstract painting with the nearly monochromatic foreground. A painterly approach seems called for. I thought some Color Scheme variations might provide inspiration. The Modern Color Scheme resulted in a higher contrast between Gary and the white wall, which works nicely.

Figure 10.24
Jazz in a gallery.

With *A Jazz Gallery* as the working title for this album, the abstract painting suggests using images derived from modern art paintings. This client has considerable knowledge of fine art from various periods, so he liked the idea of using visual references to paintings created around the time jazz was developing. The obvious place for a title is in the black area of the jacket. I'm using a font called Matisse, perfect for evoking the period and style. It will be easy to change the typeface, color, or position of this text later.

We won't use the specific painting in the photo, so let's eliminate it using some careful erasing around Gary's head followed by a Lasso selection of the remaining painting. The Delete/Backspace key gets rid of that. (Make it easier on your wrist by tilting your canvas with the Rotate Page tool.) Clean up the photo even more by taking out the microphone and whatever is on top of the piano. The image at this stage, in Figure 10.25, is ready for some jazzy artwork to be added to that white wall.

Figure 10.25
Gary cleans up real nice.

Copyright and Wrong

If you incorporate other people's work in your images without permission, be sure to change it significantly. That should protect you from a lawsuit for copyright infringement. See the Appendix for more on the topic of intellectual property.

We'll be placing three images into the background, and it would make our cutting and pasting more efficient if we could keep those images from overlapping onto Gary and the piano. This will take a few steps.

1. Make a Magic Wand selection of the clean white background. Add the brownish bits of floor to the selection by holding down the Shift key while you click in each of those areas.

2. Invert the selection so Gary and the piano are surrounded by marching ants.

3. Use the Save Selection command in the Selection menu. You'll have to name it, so call it "foreground."

4. Copy and paste a new image for the background. If it overlaps the foreground, use Load Selection and delete the unwanted pixels.

Your saved selection can be made active any time. Wondering where selections are stored? Take a look at the Channels Palette, shown in Figure 10.26, along with the full-size image with the new alpha channel visible, but the RGB (full-color) image is invisible. A channel works like a Layer Mask and can be edited by painting with black, white, or shades of gray.

You might need to see the RGB image in order to improve the accuracy of a channel. When both are visible, the channel shows up as translucent red. Repairs are still made by painting with black or white. In Figure 10.27, you see a section of the image before and after improvement.

Figure 10.26
Quiet! I'm channeling.

209

Figure 10.27

A close shave.

I chose the three images shown in Figure 10.28 to decorate the wall behind Gary. From left to right, they are a Diego Rivera, a Picasso, and a portion of a Kandinsky. Rather than have them as three images hanging separately, I plan to blend them into a mural. Figure 10.29 shows the elements in place, after some color manipulation. I applied a Chalk Drawing Color Scheme to the Rivera and increased contrast. I really like the cubist lute player by Picasso but wanted to punch up the color. The Impressionist Color Scheme did the trick. The only change made to the Kandinsky fragment was with Effects > Orientation > Distort to make it fit that odd space on the right.

Figure 10.28
Rivera had a cubist period, too.

Figure 10.29
Three easy pieces.

To Smear, Perhaps to Clone

After all that preparation, we're finally ready to do some painting!
I used Smeary Varnish from the Impasto category for the look of
thick paint with bristly brush strokes. Recall using this brush in
Lesson 5 on a portrait study and also in Lesson 8 when we created
an abstract painting and again in the animation lesson working
with the Muybridge dancer sequence. I like this variant a lot.

There is a detail showing a section of the image before and after
smearing in Figure 10.30. Use short strokes in a variety of directions, mostly following the shapes, but also deliberately blending
hard edges and dragging color from one area to another. This
stage can be pushed further, but don't obliterate the original art
completely.

The stage shown in Figure 10.31 is ready to show the client. I hope he likes the contrast between the painterly sections and the untouched photograph. The fact that his head is a painting while his hands are realistic implies a combination of styles in his music.

I'll also show him a variation or two with a different surface texture. The detail section in Figure 10.32 is the result of Effects > Surface Control > Apply Surface Texture using Paper, with Coarse Cotton Canvas selected from the Paper library. This minimizes the Impasto brush work. If the texture is too strong, use Edit > Fade to reduce it.

Figure 10.30

Unvarnished and varnished truth.

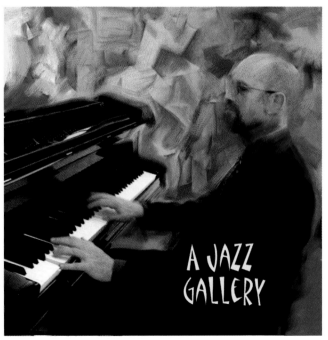

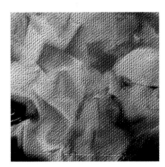

Figure 10.32

Canvassing the area.

Figure 10.31

Ready for client feedback.

Free-Style Cloning

There are no official steps for this event. Just use your favorite Cloner variants. Some of them can cover previous cloned strokes, but others must be applied to a clean area to work effectively. The Pencil Sketch Cloner, for example, needs to work on a blank area because its look relies on leaving some white spaces. Erase or delete areas as needed to redo with a different style.

I changed the background wall just a bit for the following version. The Picasso now has its original color scheme, and I switched to different Rivera and Kandinsky paintings.

Let's take another approach to the prepared collage. The painting introducing this lesson was created with a technique we can call "mixed media cloning." That is, using several Cloner variants to produce a painting with a variety of textures and brush strokes.

I began with the Spattery Clone Spray, which creates the speckled pointillist look of 19th-century painter Georges Seurat, very similar to the effect you would get if you used Clone Color with the Seurat variant in the Artists brush category. This stage is shown in Figure 10.33. Seurat lived and worked well before the jazz age, but why quibble? I'd rather scribble! That's why I chose the Pencil Sketch Cloner to redo several areas. The Oil Brush Cloner was used here and there for a few bristly brush strokes.

Figure 10.33
Play something neo-impressionist.

Unlike a fine art piece, it's easier to know when you're finished with an illustration assignment. The client tells you.

What's Next?

That's all, folks! We've finished our tour of Painter X. I hope you enjoyed the ride. Your ticket is still good if you want to go again.

A fundamentals and Beyond

In these few pages, you'll find some recommendations useful for continuing with digital painting after you're finished with this book. But first, there are a few things to discuss that will get you off on the right foot, if it's not too late.

Pixels versus Vectors

I mentioned early on that Painter and Photoshop are pixel-based. The word *pixel* is short for *picture element*, using the common abbreviation "pix" for "picture." Each pixel represents a tiny colored dot or square, and with enough of them lined up horizontally and vertically, you'll get the picture. Resolution, measured in pixels per inch (or ppi), tells you about the quality of the image. A resolution of 300 ppi has a much finer grain and more detail than the same image at 72 ppi. Resolution is especially important when images are prepared for printing. *Pixel-based* (also called *raster* or *bitmap*) images must include information on the color and location of every single one of those pixels. Depending on the dimensions and resolution, there can be thousands of such pixels in an image, resulting in hefty file sizes. For example, a Painter or Photoshop file that's 8" x 10" at 300 ppi weighs in at 20 MB. The larger the file size, the more RAM is needed and the harder your computer has to work. Older machines can really start huffing and puffing.

By contrast, *vector-based* programs, like Flash and Illustrator, are resolution-independent and have the advantage of smaller files because the image elements this time are not pixels but paths with simple fills and strokes (outlines) that can be stored as mathematical instructions. By their nature, vector-based images tend to have hard-edged lines with no thickness variation and flat color fills, whereas pixel-based graphics can have the kind of variation (called *continuous tone*) seen in photos and paintings. Working with pixels is intuitive and natural, but it takes considerable practice to get skilled at placing the anchor points and adjusting the curves that make up vector shapes.

The eyes in Figure A.1 show you the difference between pixels and vectors rather dramatically. The photo is zoomed in so you can see some pixels up close and personal. Some smears with a Blender variant made the painterly version, and it's obvious which eye was made with vector shapes. There are pros and cons to each approach, and you don't have to restrict yourself to just one or the other. If you're not sure which category you prefer, ask yourself if you'd rather have precision or instant gratification. Do you like being able to create clean, sharp lines or juicy, smeary ones? I knew I was a pixel-packin' mama from the start!

Can't We Just Get Along?

Pixel pushers can have access to some of the benefits of Vector World. In Lesson 6 you got the opportunity to work with Painter's Shapes feature. You can even open Adobe Illustrator (version 8) files that are in .ai or .eps (encapsulated postscript) format and see each shape in your Layers Palette. Of course, these vector images must be converted to pixels, or rasterized, which sounds much more exotic.

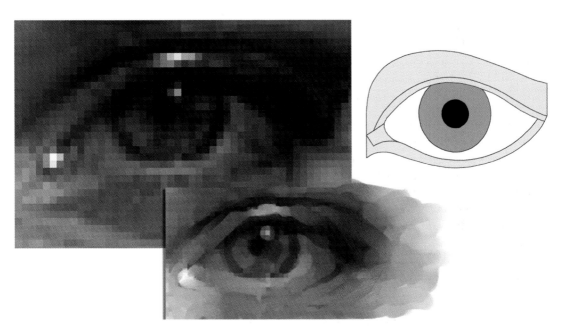

Figure A.1

To smear or not to smear—that is the question!

Take Two Tablets and Call Me in the Morning

Actually, only one graphics tablet is needed, no matter how many computers you may have. If you're shopping around for a tablet, I'll make things easier for you. Wacom Technologies is the only manufacturer to consider, and I'm not getting any kickbacks.

They make a range of tablets in several sizes for every budget and work situation, from the petite entry level 4" x 5" Graphire for $100 to the $2500 Cintiq, which is actually a monitor you can draw on. (If you can simply learn to look up at your regular screen while your pen is working down below on your desk or in your lap you can save $2400! Just look at the cursor to see where to paint. See, doesn't that prove I'm not on the Wacom payroll?)

It's easy to use a pen tablet because every point on the tablet has a matching point on the screen. When you move your pen over the tablet, the cursor moves in precisely the same way on the screen. Where you touch your pen tip to the tablet is where you click. If you need to establish or customize this "mapping" relationship, use Wacom Tablet preferences, shown in Figure A.2. This is the Mac version, found in System Preferences. The way to find Wacom prefs on a PC is as follows: click on the Start button > All Programs > Wacom Tablet Folder > Wacom Tablet Properties. These are the default settings for mapping. Notice that Pen mode is selected rather than Mouse mode. That's very important to assure the point-to-point matching of screen and tablet. You can actually specify different settings for different applications.

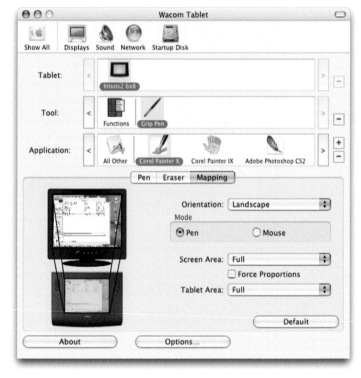

Figure A.2
Tablet Mapping settings.

Figure A.3 shows a portion of the preferences pane with the settings available for your Wacom pen. Several variables can be adjusted to customize pen behavior, including choices for the click functions of the lever on the side of some pen barrels.

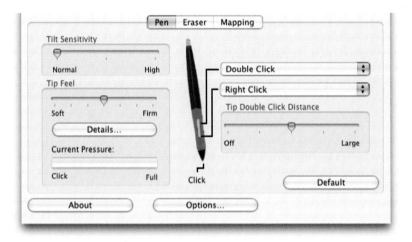

Figure A.3
Wacom Pen settings.

The Graphire tablet shown in Figure A.4 is being used for tracing an image placed under the transparent frame that comes with all tablets. This particular model is Bluetooth capable, so no pesky cord is required. You get a cordless mouse, too.

Figure A.4
Drawing hand sold separately.

My personal choice is the mid-range Intuos series, which has more levels of pressure sensitivity than a Graphire tablet. My preferred size is the very portable 6" x 8", and there are several sizes all the way up to 12" x 19". Every Wacom tablet comes bundled with Painter Essentials, the "lite" version of Corel Painter, as well as with Photoshop Elements, the stripped down version of that other pixel-based program. So you'll probably need a copy of my previous book, *Fun with Photoshop Elements* (I haven't seen a royalty check for a while).

The Wacom Web site, www.wacom.com, is as user friendly as can be, offering you help in deciding which tablet is best for you, downloads for updating drivers (software), technical support, and even a Tips and Tricks section for users of Painter, Photoshop, and Flash.

What's Your Preference?

I've already mentioned a couple of important items under Corel Painter > Preferences, especially Brush Tracking. That's where you make a test stroke to set the tablet's sensitivity to your touch. Use it when you begin a work session and anytime you feel the need for an adjustment. This is much easier and faster than using the Wacom Tablet preferences.

The General Preferences panel, shown in Figure A.5, has several settings you'll want to customize sooner or later (the sooner the better for Units). It's set at Pixels by default, but I just can't help thinking in inches, so that's what I pick. You Europeans and other civilized folks can choose centimeters. There are points and picas for you typesetters and columns for you neo-classical architects.

With Brush Ghosting enabled, the cursor becomes the shape of your current brush tip, and Enhanced Brush Ghosting (Painter X) shows the angle and direction of your pen. These options can slow you down if you're using some of the more complex brushes and your computer isn't on steroids. While your brush is moving, what do you want the drawing cursor to look like? Several choices are here, from a tiny triangle to a tiny brush icon, with color options and a choice of orientation to accommodate either your handedness or your lifestyle.

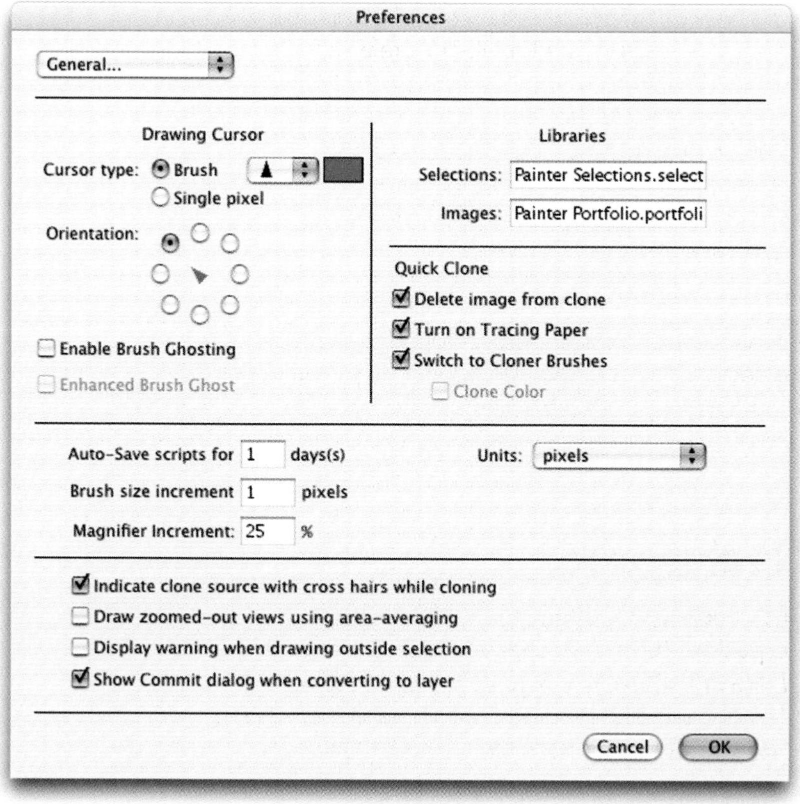

Figure A.5
Cursors and units and more.

As for Quick Clone (Painter IX and X), accept the defaults, enabling all three options. That's what makes it Quick. And if you're into quickness, you might want to change Brush Size Increment to two or three pixels so that when you use the bracket keys ([ ]) to reduce or enlarge your brush size on the fly, changes will be made more quickly. All the other default settings seem sensible, so don't change them until you feel the need.

Different Strokes

Another excellent way to increase speed and efficiency (if you're into that sort of thing) is to learn the keyboard shortcuts for the most frequently used commands. Some of these are specific to Painter, but most are used by all programs, so you might know them already. A couple of modifier keys are different for Mac versus PC users. On the Windows platform, the Ctrl key corresponds to the Command key on a Mac (that's the key with the Apple logo and the thing that looks like a four-leaf clover with an eating disorder). The Alt key on a PC is the equivalent of the Option key for Mac users. There are a few other differences, like Delete serving the same purpose as Backspace on a Mac.

Get Off My Intellectual Property!

Here's some free legal advice, and I assure you it's worth every penny.

If you scan images printed in books or magazines or search the Web for digital pictures, be aware that such items might be copyright protected. That's not a problem unless you want to publish your edited versions. Copyright law gives the original creator of an image all rights to it, including derivations thereof (or is it "wherefrom"?). How much would you have to change an image to make it legally your own and not just a derivation? Are you willing to go to court to find out?

When it comes to using the likeness of a celebrity, things can get complicated. Are you infringing on the copyright of the subject or the photographer who created the photo? Maybe both. Famous people have the *right of publicity* to prevent others from making money with their likeness, even after death. On the other hand, ordinary folks have the right to privacy, so you need to get a "model release" signed before you can legally publish their faces.

There are exceptions to copyright protection, called *fair use*. For example, you can publish doctored images of famous people for satirical purposes. Copyright expires 70 years after the death of the creator (last time I checked), after which the image becomes *public domain*, so anything goes. An image like the *Mona Lisa* is *way* in the public domain, even though the actual painting is owned by the Louvre in Paris. Ownership of a piece of art is completely separate from usage rights thereto. The images made available to you on the CD that comes with this book are provided only for your personal use in working on the projects. All other rights are reserved by the copyright holders.

Table A.1   Keyboard Shortcuts

Menu Command	Mac	PC
File > New	Cmd+N	Ctrl+N
File > Open	Cmd+O	Ctrl+O
File > Save	Cmd+S	Ctrl+S
File > Save As	Shift+Cmd+S	Shift+Ctrl+S
File > Iterative Save	Option+Cmd+S	Alt+Ctrl+S
File > Close	Cmd+W	Ctrl+W
File > Print	Cmd+P	Ctrl+P
Edit > Undo	Cmd+Z	Ctrl+Z
Edit > Copy	Cmd+C	Ctrl+C
Edit > Paste	Cmd+V	Ctrl+V
Select > All	Cmd+A	Ctrl+A
Select > None (Deselect)	Cmd+D	Ctrl+D
Select > Hide/Show Marquee	Shift+Cmd+H	Shift+Ctrl+H
Window > Zoom In	Cmd+ (plus sign)	Ctrl+ (plus sign)
Window > Zoom Out	Cmd+ (minus sign)	Ctrl+ (minus sign)
Window > Zoom to Fit	Cmd+0 (zero)	Ctrl+0 (zero)
Window > Screen Mode Toggle	Cmd+M	Ctrl+M

Resources

This section suggests sources for more training, images to play with, media to print on, and even places to display your work to other digital painters.

If you have an Internet connection, there is instant access to online tutorials and the Painter community from your Help menu. Choose Help > Tutorials to learn from such Painter luminaries as John Derry, one of the original creators of the program. Help > The Corel Classroom takes you to The Painter Canvas eNewsletter, where you can sign up for this free monthly "forum for Painter aficionados to learn new tips and techniques, to share and download custom brushes and product freebies, and to discuss all things Painter."

Browse through a few back issues in The Painter Canvas archives, then click on the Resources button in the menu strip. When you get to that page, click on Books, CDs, and DVDs to see what else is available to continue your Painter training.

When you launch Painter IX or X, don't be so quick to dismiss the Welcome screen. Use the tabs along the edges of the "open book" format to get help, encouragement, and a peek at the work of other Painter artists. The Extra Content tab, shown in Figure A.6, has a link to online tips and tricks that give you more insight into features and techniques that I might have left out or glossed over. The bottom tab, Painter on the Net, sends you to a series of Quick Tips that simply tell you what a feature does and how to access it.

Figure A.6
You're welcome.

Finding Images

If you enjoyed working with the stop-motion photos by Muybridge in Lesson 9, you might want to buy the entire collection from Dover Publications. There are two slim volumes, *Muybridge's Animals in Motion* and *Muybridge's Human Figure in Motion*, that provide not only a printed catalog showing each photo sequence but all images on a CD as electronic clip art. For only $14.95 ($22.50 Canadian), you get enough raw material to keep rotoscoping for years. Are these images royalty-free and in the public domain? You betcha—Muybridge died in 1904.

Way Beyond Disney

I mentioned the dancing hippos from Disney's 1940 film *Fantasia* when I introduced rotoscope animation. There are more recent and much more exciting examples. The Beatles' *Yellow Submarine* (1968) used the rotoscope technique in the "Lucy in the Sky with Diamonds" sequence. Brilliant colors and brush work change every few frames for a gorgeous, splashy effect that's breathtaking even if you're not taking a psychedelic substance. A much darker, gothic style is used in the rotoscoped portions of Ralph Bakshi's highly original *Wizards* (1977). Finally, Richard Linklater's sci-fi thriller, *A Scanner Darkly* (2006), is a rotoscope tour de force—every frame was drawn and painted from live action footage, yielding effects that would be impossible any other way.

You'll probably want to shoot most of your own source photos, but when you need a variety of images or something unusual in a hurry, use the Internet. If you don't mind low resolution and are careful about possible copyright issues, use Google's search engine. When you get to the Google home page at www.google.com, click on Images instead of Web and type in what you're looking for. This is a great way to get visual references for accuracy or just browse for ideas.

There are commercial online sources for high-quality stock photography. They generally require payment of fees for specified usage, and their target market is professional designers and illustrators.

If you want a lot of images, those fees can really add up. For stock images with a liberal licensing agreement at bargain prices, my vote goes to ShutterStock.com. It's easy to use their Boolean search engine to find what you need quickly, and best of all, you can subscribe for a relatively small fee, considering the volume of images you'll get. One month of this service costs $200 last time I checked, and it allows you 25 images per day or a total of 750 photos for the month. That's less than 26 cents per image. Other companies can charge $200 for a single photo! Check it out at www.shutterstock.com.

Consider using your older (analog) photos. Take old snapshots out of the family album or the shoebox and digitize them. A basic scanner is pretty cheap and is a handy device to have around. If you want to digitize images found in books or magazine, your scanner should have a Descreen feature. This is needed to prevent an unsightly *moiré pattern* from the halftone dots used in process printing. Published images are almost certainly copyright protected (not a problem if you're just using them in the privacy of your own home and with consenting adults).

Printing

I've got an inexpensive Canon PIXMA ip1600 inkjet printer that I use for most of my letter-size printing. I can get spectacular results as long as I use high-quality paper or other media to print on. Ordinary paper is too porous, letting ink spread into the fibers, so images get blurry or muddy looking. This is as good a place as any to mention that it's practically impossible to print all the vibrant, saturated color that you see on your monitor. The colors on your screen have a wider *gamut* (range) than you can achieve with ink on paper. Given the gamut limitations that come with the territory, my choice for crisp rich color is glossy photo paper. Epson and HP make it, among others. It comes in various weights and can be glossy on both sides.

For wearable art, consider printing your images on iron-on transfers that can be applied to clothing, hats, or what-have-you. Avery makes inkjet magnet sheets, which I print with several small images (like the gesture drawings I showed you in Lesson 8). Then I trim them into shapes for some unique refrigerator magnets.

Archival-quality media are available for fine art printing from your desktop. A great resource is www.inkjetart.com, where you can find letter-size or larger canvas (glossy or matte), watercolor paper, and printable fabrics. If you know you'll print on canvas, you won't need to add an optical canvas texture to the artwork.

If you want to print BIG but don't want to invest in a large format printer, order from an outfit like Imagers (www.imagers.com/poster.html). Visit their Web site for a price list of poster sizes from 18" x 24" to 59" x 96" printed on photo paper, film, vinyl, or canvas. Another company, youHuge.com, offers poster-size prints that can be mounted on foam core or other boards. Check them out at www.youhuge.com/large_format_posters.htm.

Fonts

After using the Text tool for a while, you might get a hankering for more exciting typefaces than just the ones factory installed on your computer. Lots of fonts are available free for personal (non-commercial) use. They can be downloaded from sites like Larabie Fonts (www.larabiefonts.com) or Blue Vinyl fonts (www.bvfonts.com). Use your favorite search engine to find more font resources on the Web. When I entered "free fonts" in a Google search and clicked the I'm Feeling Lucky button, what came up was the site The Ultimate Font Download (www.1001 freefonts.com). This is a collection of 6,000 "quality fonts from award winning font designers" for both Windows and Mac OS X. You can download them all with one click. Okay, they're not quite free, but at $14.95, that's a sweet deal!

If you need a special font and are willing to pay a little more for it, there are quite a few possibilities. LetterHead Fonts specializes in rare and unique fonts for artists and designers, and it charges about $30 per font (www.letterheadfonts.com). The P22 Foundry (www.p22.com) proudly announces that it "creates computer type-faces inspired by Art, History, and sometimes Science ... renowned for its work with museums and foundations to ensure the develop-ment of accurate historical typefaces...." Pretty impressive; and P22 fonts are available for as low as $19.95. Incidentally, many type houses still call themselves foundries, even though they hardly ever need to pour molten metal into molds anymore.

Fonthead Design (http://fonthead.com), sells distinctive display fonts in sets of about a dozen in volumes for $34 each. That's less than three bucks a font. Pretty good for such delights as LogJam, Shoestring, CatScratch, Cyber Monkey, and Croissant. Fonthead also offers a few freebies, including some whimsical fonts like Good Dog and SpillMilk, and a set of cartoon face dingbats (small decorative images or symbols) called Font Heads.

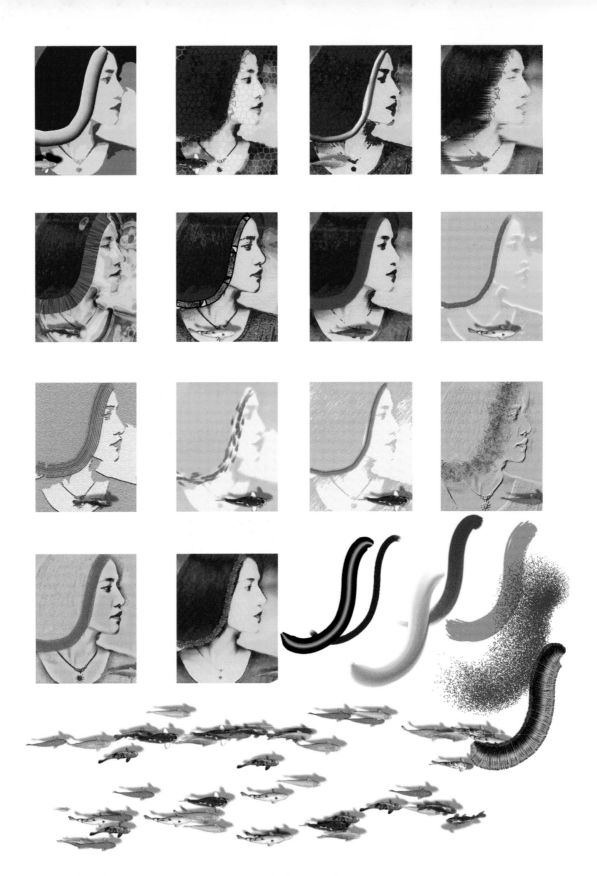

Index

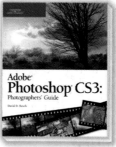
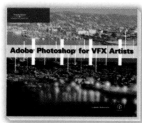

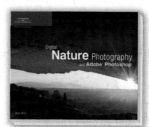

License Agreement/Notice of Limited Warranty

By opening the sealed disc container in this book, you agree to the following terms and conditions. If, upon reading the following license agreement and notice of limited warranty, you cannot agree to the terms and conditions set forth, return the unused book with unopened disc to the place where you purchased it for a refund.

License:

The enclosed software is copyrighted by the copyright holder(s) indicated on the software disc. You are licensed to copy the software onto a single computer for use by a single user and to a backup disc. You may not reproduce, make copies, or distribute copies or rent or lease the software in whole or in part, except with written permission of the copyright holder(s). You may transfer the enclosed disc only together with this license, and only if you destroy all other copies of the software and the transferee agrees to the terms of the license. You may not decompile, reverse assemble, or reverse engineer the software.

Notice of Limited Warranty:

The enclosed disc is warranted by Thomson Course Technology PTR to be free of physical defects in materials and workmanship for a period of sixty (60) days from end user's purchase of the book/disc combination. During the sixty-day term of the limited warranty, Thomson Course Technology PTR will provide a replacement disc upon the return of a defective disc.

Limited Liability:

THE SOLE REMEDY FOR BREACH OF THIS LIMITED WARRANTY SHALL CONSIST ENTIRELY OF REPLACE-MENT OF THE DEFECTIVE DISC. IN NO EVENT SHALL THOMSON COURSE TECHNOLOGY PTR OR THE AUTHOR BE LIABLE FOR ANY OTHER DAMAGES, INCLUDING LOSS OR CORRUPTION OF DATA, CHANGES IN THE FUNCTIONAL CHARACTERISTICS OF THE HARDWARE OR OPERATING SYSTEM, DELETERIOUS INTERACTION WITH OTHER SOFTWARE, OR ANY OTHER SPECIAL, INCIDENTAL, OR CONSEQUENTIAL DAMAGES THAT MAY ARISE, EVEN IF THOMSON COURSE TECHNOLOGY PTR AND/OR THE AUTHOR HAS PREVIOUSLY BEEN NOTIFIED THAT THE POSSIBILITY OF SUCH DAMAGES EXISTS.

Disclaimer of Warranties:

THOMSON COURSE TECHNOLOGY PTR AND THE AUTHOR SPECIFICALLY DISCLAIM ANY AND ALL OTHER WARRANTIES, EITHER EXPRESS OR IMPLIED, INCLUDING WARRANTIES OF MERCHANTABILITY, SUITABILITY TO A PARTICULAR TASK OR PURPOSE, OR FREEDOM FROM ERRORS. SOME STATES DO NOT ALLOW FOR EXCLUSION OF IMPLIED WARRANTIES OR LIMITATION OF INCIDENTAL OR CONSE-QUENTIAL DAMAGES, SO THESE LIMITATIONS MIGHT NOT APPLY TO YOU.

Other:

This Agreement is governed by the laws of the State of Massachusetts without regard to choice of law principles. The United Convention of Contracts for the International Sale of Goods is specifically disclaimed. This Agreement constitutes the entire agreement between you and Thomson Course Technology PTR regarding use of the software.